The ... 's of Nepal

Tales of a Grandmother - Volume 1

Audrey Forsyth

First published in 2020 byArdler Books

ISBN Paperback: 978-1-8383088-0-3
Ebook: 978-1-8383088-1-0

British Library Cataloguing-in-publication Data

A catalogue record for this book is available from the British Library

Cover design – Graham Forsyth

Published with the help of Indie Authors World

Front Cover Illustration :– Audrey discovered some beautiful arts and crafts in Lima, Peru and we brought home this decorated paper mâché, double door, front opening, container within which was hidden, also in finely worked paper mâché, a musical instrument shop complete with a large number of all types of instruments.

Photograph, Illustration and Map Credits:

General Source of Photographs 1,2 3 and 4 included in Note 4
https://commons.wikimedia.org/wiki/Category:2015_Nepal_earthquake_damage
from Wikimedia Commons, the free media repository

Attribution Photo 1 – Earthquake Damage Kathmandu

Page URL: https://commons.wikimedia.org/wiki/File:Nepal_Earthquake_(54).JPG

FileURL:https://upload.wikimedia.org/wikipedia/commons/b/b0/Nepal_Earthquake_%2854%29.JPG

Photographer: Rajan Journalist / CC BY-SA (https://creativecommons.org/licenses/by-sa/4.0)

Attribution Photo 2 – Earthquake Damage Bhaktapur Durbar Square

Page URL:https://commons.wikimedia.org/wiki/File:Bhaktapur,_Nepal_(17938609001).jpg

FileURL:https://upload.wikimedia.org/wikipedia/commons/5/53/Bhaktapur%2C_Nepal_%2817938609001%29.jpg

Photographer: Katja Ulbert from Berlin, Germany / CC BY (https://creativecommons.org/licenses/by/2.0)

Attribution Photo 3 – Earthquake Damage Basantapur Square, Kathmandu

PageURL:https://commons.wikimedia.org/wiki/File:Basantapur,_Kathmandu_44600,_Nepal_(17905836446).jpg

FileURL:https://upload.wikimedia.org/wikipedia/commons/a/aa/Basantapur%2C_Kathmandu_44600%2C_Nepal_%2817905836446%29.jpg

Photographer: Katja Ulbert from Berlin, Germany / CC BY-SA (https://creativecommons.org/licenses/by-sa/2.0)

Attribution Photo 4 – Earthquake Damage Bhaktapur Durbar Square

Page URL:https://commons.wikimedia.org/wiki/File:Bhaktapur,_Nepal_(17315387214).jpg

FileURL:https://upload.wikimedia.org/wikipedia/commons/1/15/Bhaktapur%2C_Nepal_%2817315387214%29.jpg

Photographer: Katja Ulbert from Berlin, Germany / CC BY (https://creativecommons.org/licenses/by/2.0)

Other Photographs and Illustrations – Graham Forsyth

nb. Thumbnail Photographs have been extracted from videos and apologies are given for the low resolution quality arising. These have been included because of their added visual interest point of view.

Maps: Graham Forsyth

Contents

TALES OF A GRANDMOTHER

Books have knowledge – new and old –

With photos often to assist stories told.

Your Granny Forsyth's books tell of travels past –

Adventures undertaken, panoramas vast.

Audrey chose to record her journeys all –

So that you, Mirren, may enjoy her full recall.

One Day At A Time

A Personal Divertimento
on
Nepal
A land of mountains and sherpas,
monasteries and temples,
squeezed between the high barrier
of the Himalaya and the humid
jungles of the Indian plains

April 1998

"Twenty years from now you will be more disappointed by the things you didn't do than by the ones you did do... Explore. Dream. Discover."

- **Mark Twain**

"All the books in this little series are the produce of my travels and are dedicated to each of my wonderful grandchildren, both born and unborn, who enlighten my every day. My earnest wish is that these notes and photographs may encourage them a little during their lives to grow to love travel, language, culture, history and people as I have."

Audrey Forsyth

September 2013

"Opportunity comes but does not linger" – **Nepali Proverb**

Preface

The writer of this book, Audrey, had a reserved personality, a wicked sense of humour, an astonishing intellect and a lifetime spent working as a regular primary school teacher.

So what made her produce over 10 separate comprehensive travel experience stories, unpublished in her lifetime?

This may help to explain…

Audrey Ferrier Munro Forsyth, nee Smith, was born in 1946 and brought up in the small Angus village of Kirriemuir in Scotland, which is best known as the birthplace of J. M. Barrie who wrote Peter Pan.

Their family farm inheritance had been previously siphoned off through embezzlement, before being passed on to them.

An only child her great joy was music, of which she excelled at sight reading, playing various instruments but primarily the piano in which she achieved high grades.

In 1964 she trained as a primary teacher in Dundee and it was there she met Graham, studying civil engineering, who became her husband of 44 years and whose work would take them and their family around the country.

They were married in Edinburgh in 1969; their two boys being born in the 70s.

Her teaching life included the extremes of working with children in deprived areas, whom she enjoyed being with, as well as a position of deputy headship in a girls preparatory school.

Though not a professionally trained musician her musical abilities were always fully utilised and loved by the school children whether for hymns at assembly, the musical accompaniment to all the school productions or songs in the classroom.

Her greatest relaxation was playing piano transcriptions of the great composers straight through for an hour or so.

A polyglot throughout her life she had French, Italian and Spanish as her European language base and in her final years she became highly conversant in Russian, too.

Travel was her addiction, music her passion and family her love.

Being a voracious reader, embroiderer, crossword fanatic and travel anecdote raconteur were only a few of her other interests and activities.

Ill health, however, affected her off and on throughout her married life, resulting in early retirement from teaching.

In hindsight it is likely her then symptoms along with existing health problems obscured her underlying pancreatic cancer condition which was diagnosed in 2012 and took her life in 2013.

She and Graham had done much travelling, despite her poor health, it being an opportunity for her to use her languages to full effect and enjoy the history and people of the countries visited, always scribing copious notes on all she saw and experienced.

Her terminal condition brought about a great need and urgent desire for her to put these notes into the form of a journal which she then wanted to be completed in book form for grandchildren to read as teenagers.

At this stage they had six grandchildren and two on the way. The completion of these manuscripts, 10 in all and at some cost, she achieved.

So was born *'Tales of a Grandmother'* in which all her lifelong interests in music, geography, history, language, travel and people are so deeply immersed and so eloquently and often humorously expressed.

Drafts of some of these were read and enjoyed by the nursing staff who latterly provided her medical care showing it was clear that these were of interest to a greater audience than just her grandchildren.

She would have wanted the reader to enjoy them too.

Introduction

In the preface I outlined briefly my late wife's biography and the circumstances which had brought about her research, preparation and completion of her Travelogue manuscripts.

This included the final drafts of a number of books – over 10 in all – which Audrey had hand written then dictated in order to quickly achieve a completed text.

I had supported her throughout this time both computer-wise, and proof reading in order to help her to achieve her goal.

The photo below shows her hard a work in our Perthshire garden.

Naturally her expressed wish was for me subsequently to complete these in book form with the inclusion of many of the photographs I had taken at the time of our travels, in order to illustrate her texts.

With the inclusion of some additional illustrations and maps this I have done and I have endeavoured to achieve the object of her desires.

Graham Forsyth

September 2020

Nepal – April 1998

In 1998 we decided to make a visit to the country of Nepal at the foot of the Himalaya. I had read a number of articles and stories about this elusive country, which had been pre-feudal until the 1950s and almost unknown to the rest of the world.

My curiosity was piqued, and when the opportunity of a two week visit came along, we jumped at it. Of course vaccinations and malaria tablets were 'de rigeur' as tuberculosis, leprosy and a particularly resistant form of malaria is still very prevalent in this country. We were prepared to see and hear many different peoples, landscapes, customs and languages and cultural change, but were not quite prepared for the complete assault on all senses.

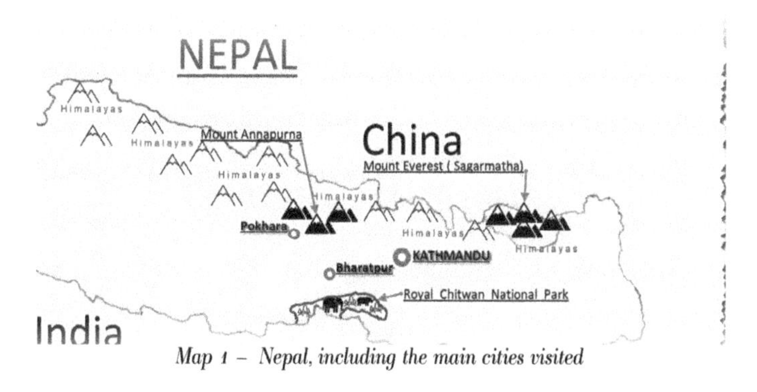

Map 1 – Nepal, including the main cities visited

Introduction and History

Nepal is such a blend of diverse countryside in a relatively small area – from the towering Himalayan peaks in the north to the sea level Terai floodplain in the south.

Himalaya is a word derived from the Sanskrit words – 'hima' snow and 'alaya' dwelling place, and the mountains contain the highest in the world and known as Everest (Sagarmatha), in Nepal and Chomolungma, in Tibet – both meaning Mother Earth – and also the next seven other highest peaks in the world.

The Terai, which is the northern most limit of the floodplain of the Ganges River (the holiest river for Hindus), is the most fertile part of the country and produces 60% of the grain for the nation.

However, this area was completely isolated until after the 1950s due to a particularly virulent strain of malaria – the dreaded 'aul', and also the desire of the ruling families to keep Nepal apart from modernisation as well as to preserve the area for their personal hunting grounds.

In between these two extremes, are the rolling Middle Hills and valleys of the country containing hundreds of ridges where farming is practised on a multitude of man-made terraces. Relentless in its ruggedness, this land still manages to provide complete food supplies for the majority of the population who are subsistence farmers dependant upon the annual monsoon rains for their survival.

The diversity continues from the crowded narrow streets of the cities (mainly Kathmandu, Patan and Bhaktapur) to the wide open spaces of the countryside, and from the marble-floored lobbies of sprawling palaces and hotels to the straw thatched mud huts, where the majority of the population live.

Due to history and early tribal divisions, this lack of contact has created dozens of different ethnic groups, each with their own languages and cultures. Religion, too, although mainly built on Hindu principles, is a real mixture with Buddhist, Animistic and Tantric elements pervading every temple.

Kathmandu, once known as Kantipar or Kasthamandap (Pavilion of Wood) originally a well-known rest house, has become the capital, and is now the political, spiritual and economic centre of the country. This flat plateau has been the scene for drama and political intrigue for centuries and dramatically, even more recently, subsequent to our visit to Nepal.

History is still a living process here where modernisation and ancient practices still vie for the nation's attention.

Ancient chronicles tell us that the Kathmandu valley was once a vast lake rimmed with mountains called Nag Hrad (Tank of Serpents) where mythical snakes known as 'nagas' guarded the treasure. Legend takes over from geology here when a Buddha tosses a seed into the water creating a lotus of a thousand petals. Then comes the Buddhisattva Manjushri who splits the mountains with a Sword of Wisdom, creating a gorge through which the water rushes out, leaving the fertile valley.

Many legends exist, and only begin to merge with historical fact, with the arrival of the Kiratis, of Mongolian origin. They were warriors whose first and greatest king, Yalambar, fought and died in the battle of Mahabharata, one of the two great Hindu epic tales.

Recorded fact appeared with the Licchavi Dynasty (AD300 -AD879) whose members were related to Indian rulers. They were a tolerant, non-sectarian people who allowed Hinduism and Buddhism to grow alongside each other. Quickly the region became a main trading centre on the borders between India and Central Asia, amassing wealth and channelling ideas between lands, adding their own unique contribution along the way.

The Valley soon became a rich tapestry of religion and philosophy and, it was in the city of Patan, that many Buddhist monks came from India, Tibet and China, to meet and exchange knowledge. When the Muslims invaded India in the 12th century, Buddhism was wiped out in its homeland and the Nepal Valley became a refuge for fleeing Buddhists and a safe haven for ancient texts.

The Licchavis were followed by the Malla Dynasty (AD1201-1768) who provided much of the art and architecture still remaining today and beginning many of the customs and festivals. Jayasthithi Malla (AD 1365-95) was the wise and powerful king, who consolidated his rule over the separate kingdoms and arranged the many indigenous Newari Tribes into 64 castes – a Hindu system.

Yaksha Malla, his grandson, was another wise and virtuous leader who ruled a stable, although controlled, society but when he died the

Valley was split between his three sons which led to much discord subsequently.

Three centuries of squabbling ensued, especially over the trade route to Tibet. Their constant rivalry, however, led to much competition between them in art and architecture. Each wanted to produce better and larger Taleju Temples, stone baths, focusing on the Durbar Squares near their palaces where virtual forests of temples abounded, and still do.

They sponsored dance, music, literature and even Tantric mysteries. Famed for their religious tolerance, they built Hindu temples and Buddhist shrines, side by side, even allowing Christians to enter in 18th century.

Although this appeared to be a stable and well integrated society for centuries, royal excesses often attained ridiculous levels. Kings would give away their weight in gold or jewels, or 1,000 cows, to Brahman priests in order to gain religious merit, as social giving was always a part of their Hindu belief to receive a better life in their next reincarnation.

However, the brutal realities of cholera, smallpox and devastating earthquakes were what the majority of the population experienced. The custom of 'sati' persisted in these parts where a widow had to join her husband on the funeral pyre after his death, and a culture of slavery was still found although in smaller numbers than other nations.

'From Chandragiri's top I asked "Which is Nepal?" They showed me, saying "That is Bhadgaon (Bhaktapur),that is Pata, and their lies Kathmandu. The thought came to my heart that if I might become king of these three cities, why, let it be so.'

Prothrombin Narayan Shah, *Dibya Uadesh. 1774.*

The future of Nepal, however, lay in the hands of the Shah Dynasty begun under the auspices of the talented and intelligent ruler of Gorkha, a central district. His name was Prithvi Narayan Shah, who turned his energy to uniting the three kingdoms of Bhaktapur, Patan and Kathmandu.

After 26 years of battles and sieges he entered Kathmandu unopposed by the drunken Newaris, during the Indra Jatra Festival in

September 1767. Over the years, the Shahs acquired more and more tribal lands until Nepal was practically the state it is today.

In1814, however, the British Raj in India became irritated by Nepal's constant nibbling away at the edges of the land and declared war. Of course Nepal lost, although the bravery of the Gurkha soldiers was noted, and the Treaty of Segouli was duly signed in 1816 demarcating the border, especially along the Terai region. A British Resident was established thereafter in Kathmandu, but he was assigned a fetid, malarial tract of land to the north of the city and the ruling family all but ignored him apart from their annual meeting.

Nepal has never been colonised by any foreign power but it has only survived by depending on the Raj and ceding large parts of the Terai but with a policy of non interference. For 104 years, however, Nepal was ruled by a Dynasty far worse than any foreign master. Jung Bahadur Rana (nee Kunwar) was young, bloodthirsty and ambitious for power.

He murdered his uncle the Prime Minister and brought about the infamous Kot massacre of 1846 where hundreds of the members of the Nepalese Court were slaughtered. He then deposed the Shah King and placed the easily controlled Crown Prince on the throne as a figurehead.

While proclaiming himself Prime Minister, and making the post a hereditary property of his family, whom he renamed Rana, claiming a dubious descent from Indian royalty. Having improved his caste, he proceeded to marry his family into the Shah Dynasty and many other royal houses.

The Queen, at the time we visited in 1998, was still a Rana. Over the next 100 years the Shah kings continued to be powerless, pampered figures who were kept well away from the politics of the country.

The Rana family ruled totally, with the national revenue providing for their sumptuous lifestyle. The Nepali people were kept in poverty, as progress was seen as a threat to the Rana's position. There was no public education, no medical care, no transport, only porters and foot tracks.

This was the case as late as 1951 because Nepal had been previously closed to the outside world, virtually a mediaeval state and with closely guarded Borders and with a national literacy of only 2%.

In the meantime, the Ranas kept in close contact with the British, in India, supplying them with famed Nepali fighters – the Gurkhas, toughened by their harsh environment – to help with the Indian Mutiny of 1857 – 58.

This steady supply of mercenaries was in exchange for non-interference and also resulted in the return of large portions of the Terai. After World War II and Indian Independence, the Ranas found themselves without the support of the British and many Nepalese, who had been in exile in India, formed political groups demanding an end to the autocratic rule of Nepal.

Audrey's own nepali cross stitch design and personal handiwork

Leaders such as B. P. Koirala and many other patriotic-minded people urged the military and popular political movements in Nepal to overthrow the Rana regime. These dramatic changes culminated when King Tribhuvan fled from his "palace prison" in 1950, to New Delhi sparking an armed revolt against the administration; he returned in 1951 as ruler presiding over a coalition government with a non-Rana Prime Minister.

Tumultuous politics ensued through the 1950s, ending with the death of Tribhuvan and the coronation of King Mahendra in 1955.

By 1957, the first free election took place putting the Congress party in government under Koirala. Only two years later, because of constant wrangling between the King and the government, Mahendra dissolved parliament and declared that a partyless 'panchayat' system would govern Nepal allowing the people a very limited voice.

This continued for the next 30 years but political abuses, corruption and suppression of dissent fuelled the growing opposition.

When King Mahendra was replaced by his son Birendra, in 1972, a referendum was held to decide whether the panchayat system should continue or a multi-party system should be introduced. The status quo won by a narrow majority, but rural communities were disappointed, and launched an agitational movement which forced the monarchy to hold the first Parliamentary elections in 50 years.

In 1991 a new constitution was established making Nepal a

"multi-lingual, multi-ethnic, democratic, independent, indivisible, sovereign, Hindu and constitutional Monarchical Kingdom".

All seemed well, but politics were still strife-ridden and corruption appeared endemic. Strikes, riots and battles between police and activists resulted. In 1996, the Communist Party of Nepal (Maoist) tried to replace the parliamentary monarchy with a People's New Democratic Republic through a strategy known as the People's War, which led to the Nepalese Civil War.

When we were there, strikes were still prevalent and everywhere in the towns and open countryside Maoist political activists were seen gathering the people into groups to hear their social policies.

Since then, of course, everything has changed. On June 1, 2001 Crown Prince Dipendra* **(Note 1)** assassinated nine members of the royal family, including the King and Queen and himself.

His brother Prince Gynanendra inherited the throne, according to tradition. However, rebellion was escalating and because of unstable governments and a siege on Kathmandu Valley in 2004, support for the monarchy began to disappear.

King Gynanendra declared "a state of emergency" in 2005 and dismissed the entire government – politicians were placed under house arrest, phone and Internet lines were cut and freedom of the press was severely curtailed.

This new regime made little progress and further strikes and protests in Kathmandu in 2006 forced the king to reinstate a seven-party coalition government which then proceeded to strip the king of most of his powers.

By December 2007, seven parties, including the former Maoist Rebels and the ruling party, decided to abolish the 240 year-old monarchy and declare Nepal a Federal Republic. Ex-King Gyanendra left the palace in June 2008* **(Note 2)** and Ram Baran Yadav became the first president.

Economically, Nepal has few natural resources and has found it difficult to emerge from a pre-feudal barter system of the 1950s into the modern age. Most are still subsistence farmers surviving on 18% of arable land who lead a very simple life.

Industry occupied only 14% but this may have improved. Nepal relies on India for imports and exports – mainly carpets and garments and although there is great potential for hydroelectric schemes only a small fraction has been tapped so far.

This diverse collection of kingdoms and tribes unified in the mid 18th century has found it very difficult to achieve a national identity with over 100 different languages and cultures. They are split mainly into two categories:

- the lowland Hindu Indo – Aryans from the south speaking a Sanskrit-based Terai and
- the highland Buddhist Mongolians from the northern Tibetan plateau speaking the Tibeto – Burman of the hill tribes.

A lingua franca similar to Hindi has been introduced and Hindu values have become mainstream overriding local customs, although they appear more relaxed about caste restrictions :-

- As in India the Brahmins, the keepers and interpreters of Hinduism, are at the top of the caste system. Their work could vary quite dramatically but they are usually well – educated and in some form of government position.
- The Chhetri have always been the warriors, enforcers and defenders, but they, too, can be in positions of power (the Rana Dynasty was Chhetri).
- The Vaisyas – in the middle, the Vaisyas are the traders, farmers and craftsmen while
- At the bottom are the Sudra or 'occupational castes' such as tailors, cobblers and smiths.

Although severe restrictions on their rights once abounded they no longer exist in law, but old prejudices will take a long time to disappear.

NEPAL – A beautiful and interesting country.

Religion in Nepal is a complex tapestry of Hinduism and Buddhism against a background of ancient animistic cults. The Newar people of the Kathmandu Valley are a prime example – formerly Buddhist but living under the Hindu-caste system since the 14th century, they have formed a unique religious synthesis.

The Nara Devi Temple in Kathmandu is a mixture of animistic goddess worship in a Hindu Tantric temple tended by Buddhist monks. Another example is the unique institution of the Kumari – a young Newar Buddhist girl, worshipped as the incarnation of the Hindu goddess Durga.

Nationally, 86% are Hindu and 7% Buddhist, but reality displays a mixture of both with ancient folk beliefs tossed in for good measure. Everywhere, deities can be found in temples, homes, mountain summits, secret ponds, rocks and trees, all taken as part of daily life and tended usually by women with gifts of red sindhur powder, uncooked rice, flower blossoms, oil lamps and incense, known as 'puja'.

In addition to this, there are the rain-making 'nagas' ie the protective serpents from folk belief twined around temple doors and statues creating a world full of invisible beings, mostly hostile, and requiring the intervention of 'jhankri' shamanistic healers to mediate.

A further complication is the addition of tantra, a mystic technique from sixth century India which has influenced both Hindus and Buddhists. Its aim is to harness energies to attain spiritual enlightenment by means of geometric diagrams (yantra), symbolic gestures (mudra) and magical syllables (mantra).

Over 5000 years, Hinduism has developed many complex cults and philosophies containing mother goddesses, powerful deities, cultural heroes, sacred trees, plants, stones, animals even incorporating monotheism.

Hindus embrace a huge number of gods and goddesses who can manifest themselves into a multitude of forms and, because their economy is cattle-based, veneration of the cow is paramount – that is why you see cows wandering freely in towns. At one time, the accidental killing of a cow held more severe penalties than that of a person. The profusion of gods is supported by a rich symbolism in Nepali art and architecture.

Multiple limbs and heads express limitless power while fiercer statues are shown trampling the helpless corpse of ignorance. In temples and shrines, each deity can be identified more easily by his animal mount – Shiva – the white bull Nandi; Vishnu – the winged bird-man Garuda; Durga – a lion; and Ganesh – a rat.

The Hindu triad of Brahma – Vishnu – Shiva has been in place since the fifth century BC, but Brahma, the Creator, is largely ignored, as in India. Shiva the Destroyer or Transformer represents vitality, change and fierce energy and can take 108 different forms – one of these is the terrifying fanged Bhairab who can only be placated by offerings of alcohol and blood. His universal symbol, the linga, distinctly phallic in origin, displays his generative power.

Nepal's special patron, Pashupati, the 'Lord of the Beast', is a remnant of early Shiva worship.

Vishnu – a much gentler deity is often depicted as Narayan, a handsome man holding a Conch shell, lotus, discus and club. He has 10 manifestations, one of whom is Krishna, playing the flute and Rama, the hero of the epic Ramayana.

Ganesh

Most popular of the deities is Ganesh, the pot-bellied, elephant-headed harbinger of luck and remover of obstacles.

Female goddesses are either compassionate and maternal or fierce and cruel – all coming from Shakti, a cosmic energy in female form. These include Parvati (Shiva's spouse); Saraswati (Brahma's consort) and Lakshmi (consort of Vishnu); while Durga, the slayer of the buffalo demon; Black- faced Kali; Chamunda – who holds the power of death; and Sutala, the dreaded smallpox goddess (now rather redundant) are some of the fiercer and scarier examples.

Buddhism does not worship a god, but the principle of enlightenment, following the example of Siddhartha Gautama, their original leader, who never declared himself as a prophet or special being.

God exists in Buddhism but is subject to karma and forces of death and rebirth.

However, more ritual has been adopted by the ordinary worshippers, and they have produced statues of Buddha and Bodhisattvas, although technically they are not deities.

Newari Buddhists have become distinctly Hinduised and worship an army of local folk deities such as the Valley's patron, Machhendranath, who appears in red and white forms and is not worshipped for enlightenment but practical things like rain, health, wealth and children.

Tibetan Buddhism has a greater emphasis on the tantric influence displayed in walls of carved stone and the many fluttering prayer flags that dot the Himalayan landscape. In Kathmandu, the Tibetan Buddhists focus on the stupas at Boudhanath and Swayambhunath, where refugee leaders have built magnificent monasteries (gompa)

Due to the diversity of religion, Nepal, of course, is crammed with festivals meaning 50 to 120 holidays per year. The official Nepali year begins in April with the festival of Bisket Jatra, where the god Bhairab and his wife Bhadrakala are hauled down curiously cobbled streets in massive wooden chariots (we were in Kathmandu visiting, at this exact time).

Going There

Sunday 5th April

Our adventure began as usual with a flight to London which was inevitably delayed, on this occasion, because of damage to the runway at Heathrow.

The rush and excitement had made me feel quite nauseous or perhaps it was the effect of the malaria tablets.

Having collected our luggage and walked to Terminal 3, through torrential rain, we duly checked in at PIA, (Pakistan International Airlines). Here our Saga rep informed us that there was a transport strike in Kathmandu and that we might have to stay overnight at the airport there. Our departure lounge was full of a multitude of different nationalities but it was quite easy to pick out our fellow Saga travellers. We had also arranged to meet our son Campbell and passed a pleasant hour chatting over a sandwich.

When it was time to board, our rep once again told us that we would have to fight for our seat, as it was pretty much a free for all once we boarded the plane – but it was not too problematic and we left a dismal wet London at 8.00pm.

As PIA is an Islamic airline, 'Inshallah', a prayer to Mohammed was said each time before take-off and before landing.

It also meant there was no alcohol on board and the food we experienced was always curry.

At about 3:00am we landed in Dubai for refuelling and were allowed to stretch our legs in the transit area. It was a beautiful new airport but the groups of black clad woman squatting on the floor made us realise that already we were heading into new cultures.

Monday 6th April

Our next stop was Karachi, in Pakistan, and by this time we were into Monday 6th of April.
Disembarkation was again obligatory, where we had to renew our boarding passes and retag all of our luggage and go through strict security checks (women went behind a screen).
It was my first experience of an Islamic airport, where the carpets were woven in the form of prayer mats, all facing Mecca.

Reboarding our Kathmandu flight and after another curry we completed the final leg of our journey across India to Nepal. We arrived at Kathmandu's Tribhuvan International Airport to a warm but dull and cloudy day. Graham immediately tried to change some Scottish pounds for rupees but was refused with a disdainful look. Passport and visa control and luggage collection all seemed calm and pretty straightforward, lulling us into a false sense of security, before we hit the turmoil awaiting us on the other side of the door.

We were met by – swarms of porters all desperate to carry our luggage; hundreds of men protesting with banners and placards; lines of rickshaws waiting for customers and a multitude of children wanting money. It was difficult to hold on to everything and also, in the chaos, to know who was officially there to meet and collect us.

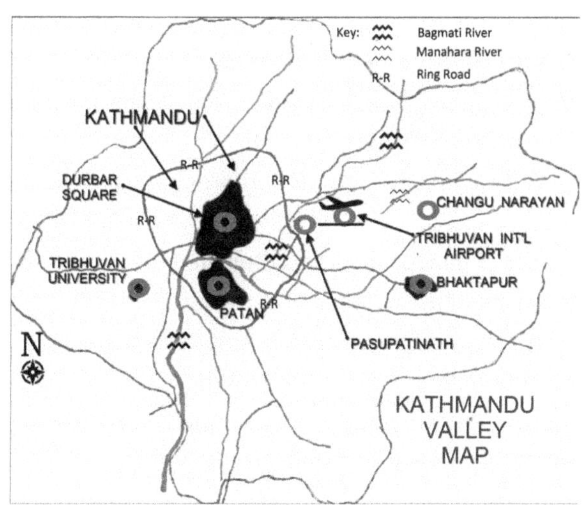

Map 2 – The Kathmandu Valley

We were greeted with 'namastes' and garlanded with prayer shawls presented to us in all directions, but eventually we discovered that an old single decker bus had been acquired to transport us, and a few other paying travellers, to our hotel in Kathmandu.

Namaste ('I salute the god within you') is the standard greeting in Nepal and is delivered with palms together as if praying. As a foreigner who is outside the complex social structure, the height of your hands is not important although our guide told me once that I was giving too much reverence to the man who opened the hotel door.

Nepalis rarely call anyone by name as they are superstitious that bad spirits might hear and plague one with bad luck.

Our tour guide, Jenny, was called 'didi' (older sister) and generally an older person is referred to as 'auntie'or 'uncle'. Garlands and prayer scarves are another common form of showing respect.

The bus we travelled in was an old army-coloured vehicle, rusty and with several holes in the floor and cracked windows full of bullet holes.

We piled on, while all of the luggage was thrown into the aisle, where it sat very precariously. I found a seat and only then realised that a Nepali soldier in battle gear and with a rifle was sitting at the window next to me.

Looking around, we had 3 armed guards to protect us from the rioting strikers. The journey was very bumpy over the rough roads and the driver kept his foot down, his hand on the horn and drove like a maniac at speed, barely missing pedestrians, cows and water buffalo.

We drove through the deserted thoroughfares belching large plumes of black smoke from the exhaust and passing, all along the 5 or 6 km, lines of glaring men, standing on either side of the road.

Having read about the strikes and riots after the event, I don't think we were aware of how dangerous the situation actually was.

The returning holiday tour group leaving on our flight had been required to travel to the airport in rickshaws, with their luggage on their knees, and in a torrential thunderstorm. We were very lucky!

Armed guards greeted us at the gates of our beautiful residence – the Hotel Malla, which was only a stone's throw away from the Royal

Palace, and owned by one of the princesses, whom we met later in the holiday.

A welcome drink of fruit juice awaited our arrival and soon we were in room 217 which had a lovely view of the garden, complete with Buddhist stupa and wandering noisy peacocks.

The marble-floored palace in which we were residing, had three individual restaurants in the main building and a Chinese restaurant in the grounds – we had the opportunity to try all of them.

Our first night was in the French restaurant and I even remember the menu: Minestrone, Truite Amandine and Tarte Tatin. A pleasant evening was passed meeting our fellow adventurers.

Tuesday 7th April

After a morning of information gathering about the places we were to see and after a quick insight into the customs and lives of the Nepalis, we were introduced to our guide, Henry Om, who would oversee our visit to Kathmandu.

Our first venture was to visit the old district of Kathmandu – Durbar Square – where a forest of pagoda shaped temples and shrines predominate. To get there we took the bus down the road we had travelled in from the airport yesterday, but instead of the silent strikers we now faced the mix of modern and ancient traffic chaos.

I can hardly remember all the monuments and points of interest indicated as I couldn't keep my eyes and mind from what I was seeing all around. Buses and taxis vied for trade alongside the rickshaws and tuk – tuks belching rancid smoke all around. Sacred cows and water buffaloes were wandering aimlessly among the snarl of vehicles and we even saw an elephant bouncing down the road towards us with his mahout perched high above the crowds.

Going round by the Narayanhiti Palace the official residence of the King of Nepal, at that time, we entered the Durbar Marg one of the premier areas of Kathmandu where many hotels and businesses are situated. At the end of this street, on a roundabout, is a large statue of King Mahendra, the father of the present King.

Veering around, we continued past the white clock-tower of Trichandra College, from the Rana-era, on our left, while on our right was the Rani Pokhari, a large artificial pond, which was created in 1670 as a shrine for a grief stricken queen at the loss of her son.

Now we were facing the huge grassy area of Tundikhel, an official parade ground, where children were playing various games of cricket. Today, however, the path surrounding the park was lined with hundreds of women holding up banners of protest while the little astrologers' stalls peeped out from the mélée advertising their services.

Our bus stopped on the Kanti Path just opposite the junction with New Road where we had to take our lives in our hands trying to cross this suicidal road, coughing and spluttering as we went, because of the pollution.

New Road was built in 1934 over the rubble of the great earthquake, and is today the shopping mecca for Nepalis wishing to buy modern imported goods from China or Thailand.

Continuing along Ganga Path, we were then in the large Basantapur Square which was filled with all types of goods – brassware, khukri knives, carpets, prayer wheels, buddha statues, clothing, household goods, woodcarving et cetera. We really would love to have stopped and looked, but our guide was moving us away from the hordes of children trying to sell us their wares or even half-naked and rather dirty 1½ – 2 year olds simply begging.

Khukri knife

It was difficult to assimilate the wealthy, gold-adorned women in silk saris walking blindly passed the filthy, starving street children, in the gutter.

Styles of Temple (Or Mandir) design

To us this was very depressing, as the children called out 'one rupee, one pen, no mother, no father' regularly in our ears. A pocketful of sweets or single rupee coins was necessary everywhere we went.

Freak Street (Jochhem Tol), which is not prime sightseeing territory, is rather a trip down memory lane, as this is where the hippy culture of the 1960s – 70s was based. Today, it is mainly filled with budget guesthouses and restaurants.

Freak Street

After this slight deviation, we arrived in Durbar Square, squeezed into two parts by the old Royal Palace, and which, for descriptive convenience, I will call Northern Durbar Square and Southern Durbar Square.

It was from here the old road to Tibet began and it is still a major crossroads and always chaotically busy.

The focal point of the northern part of the square is the Hanuman Dhoka (Gate) a brightly coloured doorway of beaten gilded metal, flanked by a pair of lions ridden by Shiva and Shakti.

Basantapur Square, Kathmandu

The Old Royal Palace, Kathmandu

Nearby stands the guardian of the Palace Gate, Hanuman, the popular monkey god, Rama's right hand man in the Hindu Ramayana epic.

A favourite patron of the Malla Kings, who like Rama, were held to be incarnations of the god Vishnu, Hanuman is draped in a red cape and shaded by a royal umbrella.

He is almost unrecognisable as his face is smeared with a thick paste of sindhur and mustard oil to protect onlookers from his evil eye.

The site of the palace may date back to Licchavi times but the present complex was built by the Malla Kings in the late 17th century with some of the most intricate and splendid Newari.

Hanuman Dhoka

The Shah dynasty expanded it and added four lookout towers at the south eastern corner and finally the Ranas left their mark with the dazzling white neo-classical facade of the Gaddi Baithak, modelled from London's National Gallery.

A hundred years ago there were about 40 to 50 courtyards, but today only about 10 remain, due to years of neglect and damage from the 1934 earthquake. Of course, the royal family moved out of the draughty, dimly- lit, low-ceilinged palace in 1886 to the more modern Narayanhiti Palace and only use the Old Palace for ceremonial and administrative purposes. (I suppose with the demise of the royal family it will now be a museum).

Just to the north of the entrance and protected by a small fence, is a small drinking tank set into the palace walls. The slab bears an inscription in 15 languages, and was carved in 1664 by King Pratap Malla, who considered himself somewhat of a linguist. It is supposed to be a poem in praise of the goddess Kali.

The story goes that if anyone can read the whole thing through, milk will gush from thc top. Two Frcnch words 'l'automnc and l'hiver' and the English word 'winter' can be read.

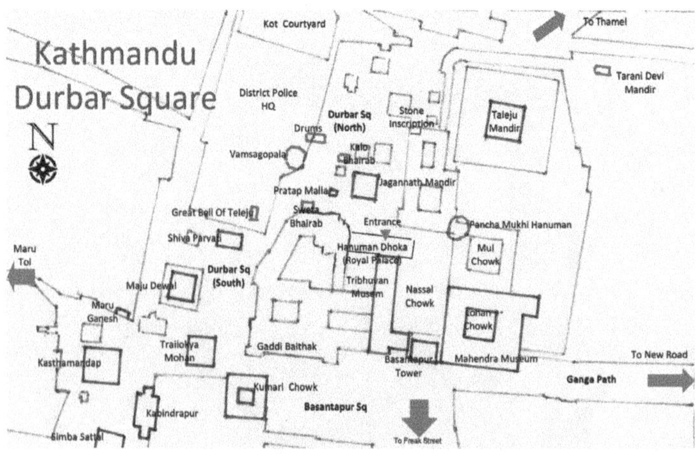

Map 3 – Kathmandu, Durbar Square

Opposite the Hanuman Dhoka is the Jagannath Temple built in 1563 in the pagoda-style and dedicated to the God, whose runaway chariot festival in India, gave us the word 'juggernaut'.

The luridly painted erotic woodcarvings at the base of the struts are the most famous in the valley, although, if you look carefully they can be found on many temples.

Jagganath Temple

Some suggested that sex is the tantric path to enlightenment but a more popular belief is that the goddess of lightning is a chaste virgin who would not dare strike temples with such carvings.

A few steps away is the towering Taleju Mandir, a pagoda set on a 12-tier plinth and built by Mahendra Malla in the mid-16th century, to outdo his rivals in Patan and Bhaktapur.

Once it was the highest building in the valley and the King decreed that no building should exceed it in height – a ban which persisted until the middle of the 20th century.

Unfortunately, this temple is only open during the Dasain festival for one day, and then only high priests, the King and the Kumari may enter.

The rest of the Northern Durbar Square is dotted with minor temples, mainly belonging to Shiva, while lying in the north-west corner is the infamous Kot Courtyard, now a police compound, where General Jang Bahadur Rana massacred 55 of the king's officials in 1846, clearing the way to make himself Prime Minister.

Nepali temples are the finest examples of Newari art. The design is over 1000 years old, as a Chinese scholar visiting Kathmandu in the seventh century described "multi storey temples so tall one would take them for a crown of clouds".

Jagganath Temple (1563) – carvings

Jagganath Temple (1563) – additional carvings

Pratap Malla

However, neglect, earthquakes and fire have taken their toll and the oldest temples still around today are from the mid-16th to the mid 18th centuries. Scholars believe that these multi-roofed towers are the prototype of the pagoda that spread across Asia taking inspiration for their form from the mountains, trees or Himalayan homes.

The builders and artists always remain anonymous but they follow a traditional form telling a story, through images and symbols. The materials of red brick and dark 'sal' wood are often lightened by lavish metal ornaments such as tinkling bells, borders of beaten metal, banners, trident and the 'patakas' – a segmented metal banner streaming down from the highest roof – as a sort of runway for divine power.

The heavy roofs are supported by massive carved struts depicting various forms of the deity which resides within and the appropriate animal mount. On close inspection smaller scenes of daily life can be seen featuring torment and erotica tapping ancient fertility symbolism. Often, a pair of protective 'nagas' – serpents – are coiled around the building forming a line between the sacred and profane.

Retracing our steps, we now returned to the Southern Durbar Square passing the great bell of Taleju on our right and the Seto or White Bhairab on our left. This enormous, terrifying ferocious mask of 1796 is thought to drive away evil spirits but the red lattice covering is only removed once a year during Indra Jatra when men jostle to drink rice beer flowing from the Bhairab's mouth.

Across the road, are a pair of immense ceremonial drums, in an open shelter, dedicated to the goddess Taleju and once beaten during worship at the temple. There was another Bhairab in the Northern Durbar Square, which I forgot to mention, again a rather terrifying sight, the Kalo Bhairab, black and luridly painted. The people from the hills remain in awe of this as supposedly anyone who tells a lie before the statue will vomit blood and instantly die.

Returning back south, this part of the square is studded with some grand but inactive temples such as the Shiva Parvati Temple with its brightly painted wooden images peering from an upstairs window. Of note, is the massive stone Garuda, the winged-bird man vehicle of Vishnu and behind this the broad roofed building of the Kasthamandap (Pavilion of Wood), the ancient temple-come-rest-house which gave Kathmandu its name and is thought to be one of the oldest buildings in the world-travellers still sleep here at night.

Before I continue to describe the buildings we saw, I must just mention that these were only a small part of what our eyes, noses and ears were experiencing.

All around and at every moment, our attention was caught by the sights, sounds and smells of Nepali life. The rich silks and gold bracelets of the well-to-do here are offset by the more common course, red and black, of the cloth saris of the Newari women and the distinctive waistcoats of the men. Then there are the richly woven aprons and colourful hats of the Tibetan people with the old constantly turning their prayer wheels in their hands.

The maroon and yellow robes of the Buddhist monks and nuns as they rush by in the street; the red and yellow costumes of the ever smiling Sadhus with their matted dreadlocks and all the time in the world; the vermilion tikas on every Hindu forehead and the red and yellow pujas made at every shrine; and the fluttering multi-coloured prayer flags all mixed with the earthy dark colours of the buildings which looked as if they would fall over on top of you at any moment, all adding to the visual richness surrounding us.

Living is done on the street, cooking on little stoves; washing and shaving; hair-cutting; traders selling or creating their goods; the Newari country people with their yokes and balance pans. containing spices, nuts and the biggest cauliflowers I have ever seen; women praying and men sleeping or playing cards; dentists pulling teeth; policemen walking around holding hands; soldiers marching; living, working, celebrating and dying – it was all happening before my eyes.

Then it was time to close one's eyes and listen:-

- the bells tinkling at every shrine
- the chatter of the traders
- the chanting of the monks
- the political speeches at every corner
- the barking of the hundreds of dogs
- the plaintive notes of a flute
- and the incessant bleating of the goats tied up at temples.

Animals abounded round every alleyway – dogs, goats, sacred cows lumbering along, large monkeys jumping from roof to roof and the odd drowsy snake trying to escape from a Saddhu's basket, along with the overpowering smell of incense, the rotting roadside garbage and pervading whiffs of raw sewage – whether human or animal I don't know.

With all this bombarding my very being, I am surprised that I remembered anything the guide was saying, however, here we were

Jagganath Temple

at the Kumari Chowk or Ghar, ie the gilded cage of the young Newari girl worshipped as an embodiment of the Hindu goddess Durga.

Built in the style of a Buddhist 'bahal', it is adorned with elaborate wood carvings and nowhere illustrates more the adaptable nature of religion in Nepal with its blend of Hindu, Buddhist and folklore elements. The last Malla King, Jaya Prakash, is said to have instituted the practice when he built the Kumari Chowk in 1757 in an act of atonement for some sexual indiscretion.

There are 11 Kumaris in the valley, including 4 in Kathmandu, 3 in Bhaktapur and 2 in Patan, but the most important is the Royal or State Kumari. Although she is supposed to be a Hindu goddess, she is chosen from the Buddhist Shakya clan of goldsmiths at about the

Kumari Chowk

Taleju Mandir (16th Century)

age of 3 to 5 years. She is meant to exhibit the '32 perfections' and, once chosen by the selection process, a large ceremony on the eighth day of Dasain, is her final test.

100 buffalo and goats are slaughtered in the old courtyard of Mulchowk while men in demon masks parade around making scary noises. If the girl shows no fear, and her horoscope does not conflict with the king's, she will become the next Kumari.

She is dressed in red, adorned with golden jewellery and her eyes are rimmed with kohl. Then she proceeds to walk to the Kumari Ghar on a strip of white cloth as her feet should never touch the ground.

Her cloistered life is spent on the second floor, separated from her family, and cared for by attendants, only being carried outside on her throne during Indra Jatra and three or four other times a year. Seated on her gilt throne her slightest action is taken as an omen;

- if she smiles the worshipper will experience good fortune
- if she is restless that is a sign of bad luck
- and if she cries or rubs her eyes it portends death

The Old Royal Palace

Royal Guard marching through Durbar Square in front of Shiva Parvati (under repair)

Malla Hotel

This charmed life continues until the Kumari sheds blood – either a cut, a lost tooth, or, more usually, menstruation, whereupon she is retired on a modest state pension and returned to a family she hardly knows. Sometimes a marriage is arranged but few find a husband since tradition rumours that husbands of the ex-Kumari will always die young.

We, being non-Hindus, were only allowed into the inner courtyard, but as I was taking a photograph a red image appeared behind the latticed windows.

Temples

Stepping out from this building, whose purpose seems quite alien and rather cruel to our culture, we came across a small but very important shrine, the Ashoka Binayak or Maru Ganesh, the home of the elephant-headed Ganesh who brings good luck and avoids trouble.

Crowds are always circling it and ringing the bell. Across the way is a larger-than-life brass image of Ganesh's trusted mount, the rat.

Making our way into Maru Tol, we saw something like a giant Christmas tree or Maypole about 60 to 70 feet high, leaning against a building and, on enquiry, discovered that it was part of the annual ritual of the great god Machhendra.

All through the increasingly hot Spring season, this large unwieldy structure with massive wheels, is pulled by groups of men heaving the wooden chariot along whilst others, holding ropes also attached

Red Machhendra Festival

to it, guide it vertically between overhanging buildings, cables and over the narrow, windy and bumpy cobbled streets.

Above the wheels is a chamber containing the deity overlaid with plates of copper gilt and surmounted by a metal umbrella with streamers and ribbons.

Usually, this annual journey is accompanied by crowds of celebrating devotees and bands playing loud strident music.

Today, however, only police and workmen were busy trying to dislodge the huge bamboo pole which had become jammed into the upper storey of a nearby building.

This area was more like a vegetable and spice market as mainly women displayed their fruit, vegetables and nuts. Here we experienced the first paan or betel leaf sellers which were extremely popular with the passers-by.

Paan or betel is a digestive and mild stimulant chewed by many. The paan wallah spreads 4 basic ingredients onto the betel leaf: katha, which gives the red colour to the mouth; supaari, chopped areca nut; mitha masala (sweet spices); and chuna (slaked white lime). It has been found recently that this constant chewing of betel can cause mouth cancer.

Another strange coincidence occurred when I discovered a lady selling sprigs of southern wood, distinctive by its smell. I asked Henry about this and he said it was to keep the evil spirits away. This was most curious, as my grandmother insisted in having a southern wood plant in the garden, (she called it 'apple-ringy') in order to keep the devil from the door. Continents apart but similar superstitions!

After wandering around for some time, we met our guide and group under a venerable old tree called Pipal Bot before returning, quite overwhelmed, to our hotel for another talk, dinner and drinks and a welcome rest.

Wednesday 8th April

Up early, today to our usual natural yoghurt breakfast – (supposed to keep the gastric bugs at bay) and then off for a drive to Bhaktapur and on up to Tilkot in the hills. Although it was early in the morning, daily life was well underway on the roads through Kathmandu. We noticed that almost every building has a shop or business located on the ground floor, where men were either sewing on their old Singer machines or sorting large bags of kapok, having a haircut or a morning shave.

Women were sweeping the side paths (I can't call them pavements) while others were carrying large panniers of vegetables and baskets of pulses into the city, having left their hillside homes at an unearthly hour. Children in smart uniforms and gym slips were on their way to school while their younger siblings toddled dangerously close to the road. A colourful display of saris, dhotis and western dress were varyingly surmounted by Chinese, Mongolian and Indian features.

Two policemen in smart blue uniforms and masks for the pollution were guiding the traffic at a roundabout, while still holding hands, and football and cricket were already in full swing in the park. A worrying sight, however, was the long queue outside the local tuberculosis hospital. All types of transport were rushing about, especially richly painted buses, with all the men sitting on the roof.

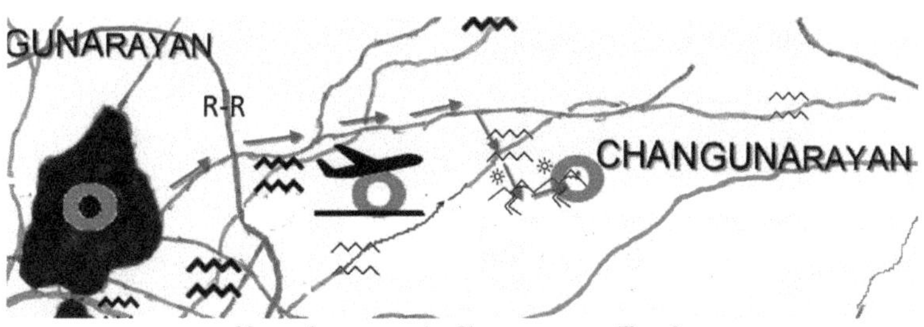

Map 4-Journey to the Changunarayan Temple

Once away from the city environs, our road became filled with goats, chickens, water buffaloes and the ubiquitous cows, while passing huge brick works and a lush green golf course completely out of place.

Soon we were in the countryside and, once stopped, disgorged from our coach to walk up the hills and along one of the many ridges leading to the ancient pilgrimage site of Changunarayan.This was the best time to go climbing before the sun was too hot, and it was a very pleasant and interesting way to spend a morning. We met many women carrying huge bags of leaves and twigs and also stumbled across groups of men having meetings in the woods – a sight which troubled our guide Henry.

Changu Narayan Trail and Temple View

Little did we know but these were Maoist activists, who often held tourists to ransom.

There were only a few villages on our route where grandmothers tended babies in swinging cradles or weeded their cabbages on the many terraces, but our presence was soon detected and, in no time, we were surrounded by groups of children looking for sweets or chocolate or even just wishing to practise their English.

On this hillside, the views from the village were spectacular, looking over the valleys, where the River Manohara sparkled in the sunlight, seemingly miles below.

As our eyes followed the main route to Tibet, we could see the snow glistening on the high Himalaya and, about lunchtime, we spotted the village of Changu and its temple far in the distance.

At the abrupt end of the ridge north of Bhaktapur, this ancient temple complex commands an extraordinary view of the valley in three directions and is delightful, after Kathmandu's noise and smog.

Despite its historical significance it is little known and rarely visited.

Percival Landon wrote in 1928:–

"One remembers all the wealth of carving of the rest of the Valley, but when all is recalled, it is probably to the shrine of Changu Narayan that one offers the palm.

Perhaps one drives back home from Bhatgon more full of thought than from any other expedition to the many outlying places of this crowded centre of holiness and history and art."

(Percival Landon "Nepal" Constable & Co London)

Various views on the walk to Changu Narayan

The route to Changa Narayan

Protected by its remote location, the pilgrimage site of Changu Narayan has changed little since this was written.

Whilst having a quick packed lunch, we watched the children and men all looking intently down a hole that was being dug (nothing changes) while the women chased the goats from their vegetable gardens.

We now climbed the large number of steps which took us through the still mediaeval village of Changu – which means 'shaking or swinging hill' – where we could see the traditional village open water conduit being used for everything; washing clothes and dishes or even just for playing by the younger children – the water was absolutely filthy.

Women taking a well earned rest were sitting on doorsteps picking nits out of each other's hair and here mange-ridden, flea bitten dogs barked at our heels all the way, but to reach the Valley's oldest Vaishnava site with its priceless sculptures was well worth it.

Habitation on the way to Changu Narayan

Dating back to the 4th century AD or even earlier, this supreme example of Nepalese architecture stands atop the hill with a main temple, rebuilt around 1700, in a quiet courtyard surrounded by rest houses and pilgrim's shelters.

The classical broad-roofed pagoda is richly decorated with painted woodwork, intricate carvings and extravagantly gilt repoussé work on the main doors.

A measure of the temple's importance is the exaggerated size of the four traditional emblems of Vishnu- the wheel (chakra), conch (sankha), lotus (padma) and mace (gada) mounted on pillars at its four corners.

A gold-plated image of Vishnu is reported to be kept inside but only Temple priests are allowed entry.

Legend says that the statue sweats miraculously, at times, indicating Vishnu is battling with 'nag' spirits and the cloth used to wipe the god's brow is considered a charm against snake bites.

Vishnu Vikrania

Changu Narayan Village and Temple which can be seen on the skyline to the right

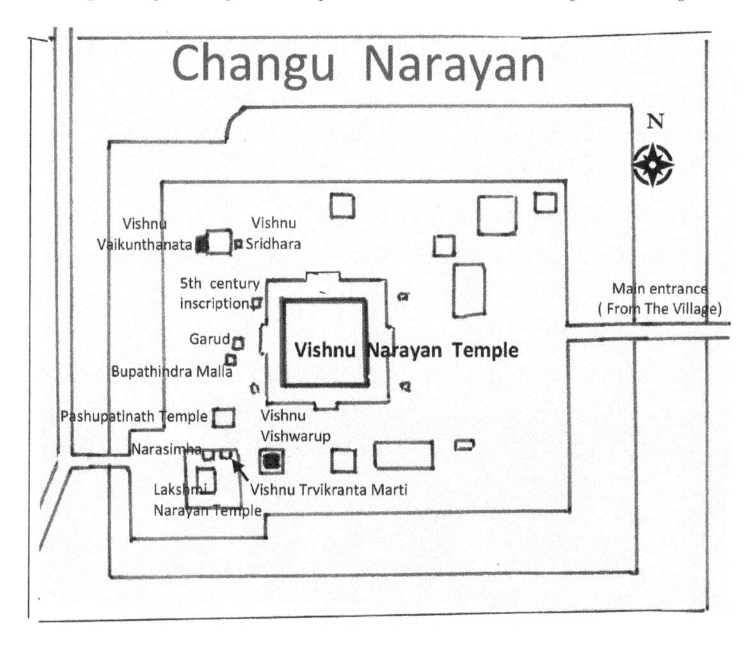

Map 5 – Changu Narayan (See Notes 3 and 5)

The pillar with the Chakra was erected over 1500 years ago by order of Manadeva, a Licchavi King.

The ancient inscription narrates how Manadeva entreated his mother not to go to 'Sati' at the death of his father.

'Sati' is a bygone practice requiring a wife to follow her dead husband to his funeral pyre and so burning alive. The Queen Mother Rajyavati did not go to Sati, after all.

Smaller temples in the compound are dedicated to Lakshmi, Kali and Shiva. Several images are scattered around this outdoor museum and, with few exceptions, all pertain to Vishnu or his faithful carrier, Garud.

A plump statue of Garud kneels before the temple looking human except for a pair of wings and a cobra scarf – it used to be mounted on a pillar. Nearby the brass statues of King Bupathindra Malla and Queen Bhuvanlaxmi are visible behind a screened cage.

The Queen was responsible for the reconstruction of the temple 300 years ago, following a great fire.

Three statues are worth noting:

- The Vishnu Vikranla striding across the universe aboard the winged Garud;
- The Vishnu Vaikunthanata which is featured on the back of a Nepalese 10 Rupee note; and
- The 8th Century Vishnu Vishvarupa inspired by the Mahabarata, with 10 heads and multiple arms, below which is an image of the Sleeping Vishnu floating on the cosmic ocean.

Two other points of interest were a Chautara and Parijat. This is a resting platform around a coral (parijat) tree – one of the five trees

Changu Narayan – Vishnu Narayan Temple

from paradise.

The other is an unfinished elephant carving. Long ago when the craftsmen were carving this for the south gate, it could not be done in one day.

When they came back to work the next day, it had moved to this location overnight and when they began to carve once more it bled – it was left untouched and attained a god image status.

As we stumbled down the hill our guide told us about the legend of Chinnamasta and Keleswar and why Changu was called the 'shaking or swinging hill'.

"Very far back in time, a demon through severe penance, was able to get a boon from Lord Siva that he could not be killed by anybody.

In due time, he terrorized all the living beings so much that they all went to seek safety from Lord Vishnu, the perpetuator of human wellbeing.

When Lord Vishnu came to wage war with the demon, his adversary even cut off the wings of Garada, his mythical bird carrier.

As Vishnu learnt of the boon and that only the primal goddess is able to kill the demon, he went into hiding in the Changu forest.

As the search for Vishnu failed, the demon picked up the hillock itself and started shaking it vigorously creating great panic.

Again Lord Mahadeva intervened and drove a long thick stake through the hillock to fix it firmly to earth and the demon could not shake it anymore.

Still today the stake is worshipped as Siva in the temple of Kileswor, located in the courtyard."

Changu Narayan Temple

The road down the hill was dreadful and our vehicle was used like a road-roller to flatten piles of material into the holes before we could continue.

Further view from the Changu Narayan trail

Our visit was completed by a trip to a shop containing beautiful pashminas and lovely turquoise and lapis jewellery.

Tonight we dined at the Imperial Palace a Chinese restaurant at the edge of the hotel grounds and this was the first time that we saw the Himalaya shining in the evening sun.

Thursday 9th April

An even earlier rise was on the cards today as we left the hotel at 5:45 am for the Domestic Terminal of Tribhuvan Airport. After receiving a tika of vermilion powder on our foreheads, we boarded an 18 seater Buddha Airlines plane (Note 5) for our flight to the Himalaya.

Tikas are the universal symbol of Hinduism, common to men, women and children. Usually comprising a mixture of yoghurt, rice and sindoor powder, the tika is a mark of blessing from the gods and an acknowledgement and representation of the divine within us all.

It is also an invocation of divine protection for those receiving it, especially on arrival or departure in aeroplanes.

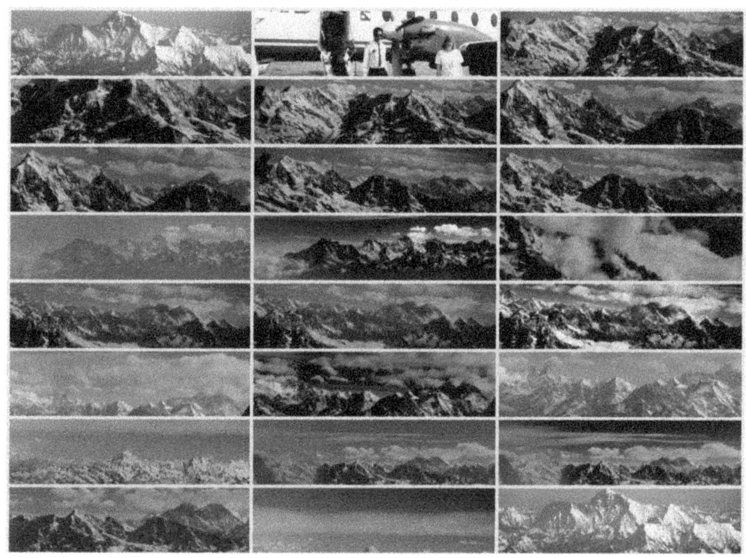

Aerial views of The Himalaya

Map 6 – Roundtrip flight on Buddha Airlines to Mount Everest (Sagarmatha)

We were off to view the Himalaya at close range in a little plane.

These mountains stretch all across the northern border of Nepal. At altitudes of over 3,000 m (10,000 feet), the Himalaya make up 25% of Nepal's land area. There are few real valleys and most rivers run through deep gorges.

There are eight peaks over 8,000 m (26,326 feet). These are Everest (Sagarmatha), Kanchenjunga (K2), Lhotse, Makalu, Cho Oyu, Dhaulagiri, Manaslu and Annapurna.

Mount Everest – Sagarmatha

Himalaya – in the clouds

About 10% of Nepal's population live in this high area. Cultivation is possible up to about 4,200 m (13,821 feet) and the main crops are potato, millet and barley, although the people who live in this area are mostly semi-nomadic, keeping large herds of sheep and yak.

The Sherpas, Nepal's most famous ethnic group, probably migrated from eastern Tibet. They were originally nomads but, with the introduction of the potato, they began to settle in villages.

Sherpas maintain the highest permanent settlements in the world – up to 4,700 m, which accounts for their renowned hardiness at altitude.

Their mountaineering talents were discovered in 1907 and, by the 1920s, hundreds were signing up as porters on expeditions to Everest and other Himalayan peaks – from the Tibet side, ironically, as Nepal was closed to foreigners at that time.

When expeditions were finally allowed into Nepal, in 1949, the Sherpas took over the lion's share of portering and four years later Tenzing Norgay reached the top of Everest clinching the Sherpa's worldwide fame.

Like Tibetans, Sherpas are devout Buddhists and most villages support a monastery and colourful prayer flags are seen everywhere.

In 1849, while taking measurements from the plains of India, members of a survey team logged a previously unnoted summit which they named Peak XV. Three years later it was revealed to be the world's highest mountain and it was named after Sir George Everest head of the Survey Team 1823 – 1843.* (Note 4)

Buddha Air Flight

Politically off limits until the early 20th century, the first attempt to climb to the summit from the Tibetan side was by a British party that included George Mallory.

Two years later Mallory and Andrew Irvine reached 8,500 m without oxygen – before disappearing into a cloud – their bodies were never found. Several attempts were made up to World War II and further problems arose when the Chinese invaded Tibet in 1950, closing the northern approaches.

In 1951, however, a race took place between the Swiss and the British, on the southern slopes. The mountain was finally scaled by New Zealander Edmund Hillary and Sherpa Tenzing Norgay in 1953. On the morning of May 29th Hillary planted the Union Jack, the Nepalese and the United Nations flags on the summit, while Tenzing left an offering of sweets and biscuits to the mountain's gods.

Often the peak of Everest is shrouded in mist, but today we were lucky, as only a few wispy clouds floated by.

Tourists often ask Nepali pilots why their flight gets delayed
or cancelled on cloudy days. A typical Nepali response is:
"Our clouds have rocks in them"

The Himalaya

Mount Everest (Sagarmatha)

The Majestic Himalaya

It was difficult to imagine the height of these snow-clad peaks, but I am so glad we took the opportunity, as we could never have seen them any other way. We were allowed into the cockpit to take a closer look and also take some photographs.

Mount Everest – Sagarmatha

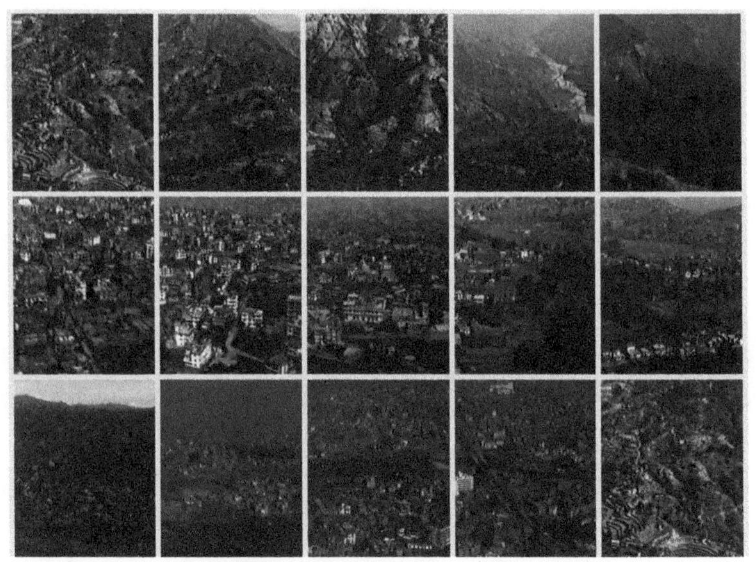

Aerial Views of Kathmandu and surrounding valley

It was an amazing sight. The pilots, of course, were more worried about crossing over into Chinese airspace, as half the mountain lies in Tibet.

We were back in the hotel by 10.00 am and passed the rest of the morning writing postcards in the hot sunshine. At 1.00 pm we went into Kathmandu with Henry Om to visit the Federation of Business and Professional Woman, Nepal, a pioneer social and professional organisation.

Since it's inception in 1975 it has been providing a link and forum to voice the interests and problems of working women, in particular, and Nepalese women, in general. The courses offered range from secretarial, to marketing, to food processing and preservation.

A literacy programme and scholarships are also being provided for diligent girls who belong to economically deprived groups. Here we met a group of young women doing a marketing course, all on computer, and a group of graduates doing an English language course. Tea was served as we chatted about life, work and family – a most insightful meeting.

Later we made our way to a local nursery which was basically two large rooms: one for babies and toddlers; the other for 3 to 4 year olds

– all dressed in their smart uniforms. The children were amazing-they could recite the English alphabet and knew all their numbers.

Pre-sleep time

After a small concert and a monetary contribution we left to the farewells of a lovely little group. Tonight, we were to enjoy a Nepali meal in the Playa Restaurant with lots of spicy and unrecognisable food.

Nearly seeping time

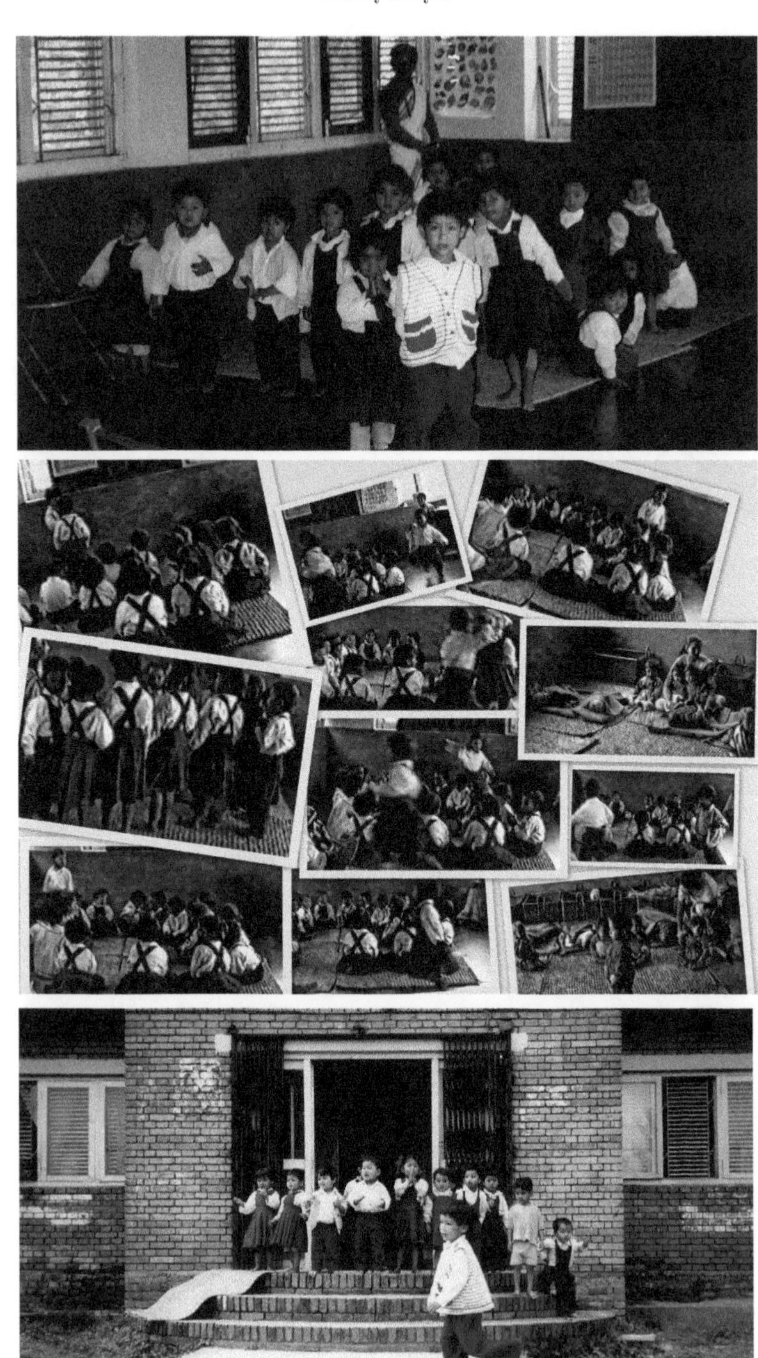

Happy nursery children

Afterwards a group of musicians on drums and flutes entertained us along with dancing and the appearance of a 'yeti'.

The yeti (man of the Tibetan folklore for centuries.) Stories of hairy-like creatures roaming the snowy heights came to the attention of the rest of the world during the early days of British rule in India.

Explorers in Tibet reported seeing mysterious moving figures leaving large unidentified footprints in the snow. On hearing these stories Fleet Street coined the term "the abominable snowman", but it wasn't until 1951, during the Everest expedition, that climber, Eric Shipton, took clear photographs of yeti tracks.

There has been plenty of circumstantial evidence, but not one authenticated sighting. Yet yaks continue to be mauled, and Sherpas insist the yeti isn't a hoax. Perhaps we want it to exist, like the Loch Ness monster – some secret part of the world that mankind hasn't yet discovered and explained.

Friday 10th April

Today, we deserved a long lie in and did not have breakfast until 8:30 am, as we were going to explore the Thamel District, just round the corner from our hotel.

Malla Hotel Gardens and Stupa

To stroll through here is to run the gauntlet with our eyes ricocheting between carpets, bookshops, jewellery and displays of prayer wheels, while dodging hustlers all the while.

Nepal offers an abundance of unique goods and the sheer quantity can, at times, be overwhelming. It is best to restrain buying until you can differentiate between the commonplace and unique and get a feel for the prices.

Bargaining is essential, a leisurely process meant to be a friendly, yet strategic game – we were not very good at it. Carpets, gilded statues, woodcarving, textiles, clothing and pottery are all available in the Thamel.

Old Newari painters produced intricately detailed Tibetan style 'Thangkas, and 'paubhas'. Thangkas are painted on flat scrolls and focus on religious themes, generally Buddhist.

They use fine lines and brilliant colours to depict Buddhist deities or the geometric designs called 'mandala'. We were very tempted but opted for a couple of water colours instead.

While Kathmandu is not a major gem-buying centre, it does offer bargains in semiprecious gems and worked silver and here I was tempted and bought one or two small pieces.

Of course, we could not leave Nepal without a Khukri, the curved knife wielded by the Ghurkas.

Some are elaborately delicate whilst others are simple and unembellished- we even had soldiers trying to sell us the ones they were wearing.

The heat and smell in the Thamel was overpowering as we passed piles of rotting garbage, butchers shops where the slaughtering was done on the road-side, and the constant dust and fumes from the tuk-tuks travelling at break neck speed.

Our trip was cut short, however, as I had a dose of the 'Kathmandu Trots' probably arising from the spicy Nepali food, the previous evening.

An afternoon of rest and recuperation followed as we enjoyed the hot sunshine. Good company and an excellent meal completed a much quieter day.

Saturday, 11 April

Off down the Thamel we went once more to pick up some of our purchases and make a visit to the Kathmandu guesthouse. Thamel's original guesthouse is still the best, set well back from the noisy street and with a lovely garden.

Nearby is the Pilgrim's Bookshop with a delightful garden restaurant and indoor cafe. Graham also bought a couple of bottles of Bordeaux from a very, very small supermarket, to reciprocate with some new acquaintances. It turned out to be undrinkable.

This afternoon we set off for the ancient city of Patan or Lalitpur (City of Beauty) its old name. Now largely absorbed by Greater Kathmandu, this once powerful independent kingdom is so different in character.

Although Kathmandu's Durbar Square is only 2 ½ miles away, the cities are worlds apart. While the Kathmanduites are amassing wealth and power, Patan's population appreciate the finer things in life.

Above all, it remains a proud city where artisans and the sounds of tapping and filing ring out from the metalwork ateliers all over the town. Urban sprawl has gobbled up the farmland between the two cities with only the Bagmati River still dividing the neighbourhoods.

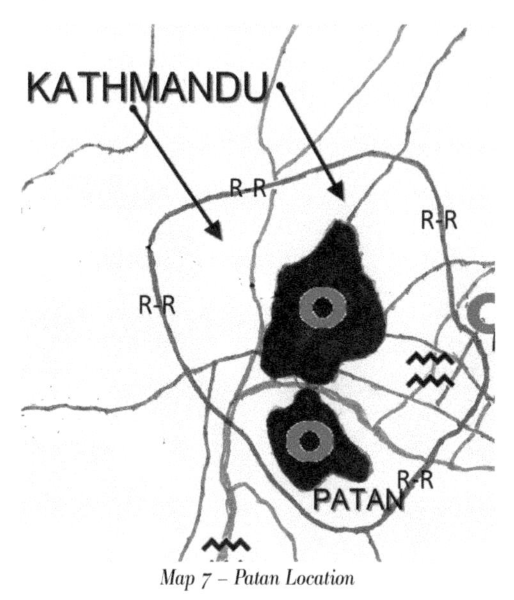

Map 7 – Patan Location

Sights of Patan

Patan has a long history as one of Asia's greatest Buddhist centres and this can still be seen in the many 'bahal (courtyards), chaitya (stupas) and shrines scattered about the town, many in danger of collapse, unfortunately.

In both legend and fact, Patan is the oldest of the 3 kingdoms in the Valley and rose to prominence when Kathmandu was only just a collection of villages.

The 'Ashoka stupas' set at the cardinal points of the old town are attributed to the visit of the Indian Emperor Ashoka in the 3rd Century BC. Historians are sceptical about this visit although the white domes on the grassy hillocks are undoubtedly very old.

Patan Durbar Square viewed from Mangal Bazaar

By the 17th Century, Patan emerged as the cultural capital of Nepal where Indian, Chinese and Mediaeval Patan was a large and wealthy kingdom and when the Malla Kings ascended the throne, they brought Patan to its full glory – most of the monuments and temples date to the 17th century.

Durbar Square, Patan

When Prithvi Narayan Shah and his Gorkhali band conquered the valley, they chose Kathmandu as their capital and Patan was largely forgotten.

Economically, this was detrimental but to the historian an absolute delight as much of the centre is still frozen in time.

Patan's Durbar Square, although smaller and quieter, still has a perfectly balanced forest of temples, pagodas, massive bells and statue-topped pillars.

It appears to be more refined, perhaps, because the city of artisans has a better eye or maybe just that it was free of meddling monument-building Kings.

As Hinduism took control, the Buddhist priesthood became a hereditary caste and the Bahals turned into trade guilds of families sharing the same caste and profession.

Our guide took us to a rooftop above the intersection of Mangal Bazaar where we had a splendid view of the Square's bell-fringed pagoda roofs, with the snowy mass of Langtang mountain in the background.

The richly decorated Old Palace stretches down the east side of the square pierced by doors leading to central courtyards. The first, the Sundari Chowk (Beautiful Square) is flanked by statues of elephant-faced Ganesh and Hanuman, the red smeared Monkey King.

The next wing, the Mulchowk, the oldest courtyard served as the residence for the royal family and is dedicated to the Malla's patron goddess, Taleju.

Lumjyal Chowk, 'Courtyard of the Golden Window' is named after its splendid gilt entrance.

Just north of the palace is Manga Hiti, an ancient sunken water tap, still in use, where women and girls fill up their metal jars.

Going back south once more, we found the octagonal stone Chyasin Dewal, opposite the Sundari Chowk, which is the lesser of the square's Krishna temples.

Some say its shape refers to the 8 wives who committed sati on the King's funeral pyre, but Krishna temples tend always to have 8 sides to commemorate Krishna's role as the eighth incarnation of Vishnu.

The cast iron Taleju Bell was the first to be erected in the valley in 1736 but Kathmandu and Bhaktapur soon followed suit due to their civic rivalry.

Sundari Chowk

Next is the Hari Shankar Mandir dedicated to both Vishnu (Hari) and Shiva (Shankar) while the statue on the pillar is Yoganendra Malla.

An angry cobra rears up behind the King's head with a gilded bird perched atop.

He kneels in prayer facing the Palace's main Taleju Temple and the cobra image is said to appease the 'nag', animist snake spirits who bring forth the rain.

Patan Temples, Bells and Manes (Prayer Wheels)

This 17th-century king renounced his throne after the death of his favourite son and became a wandering Saddhu.

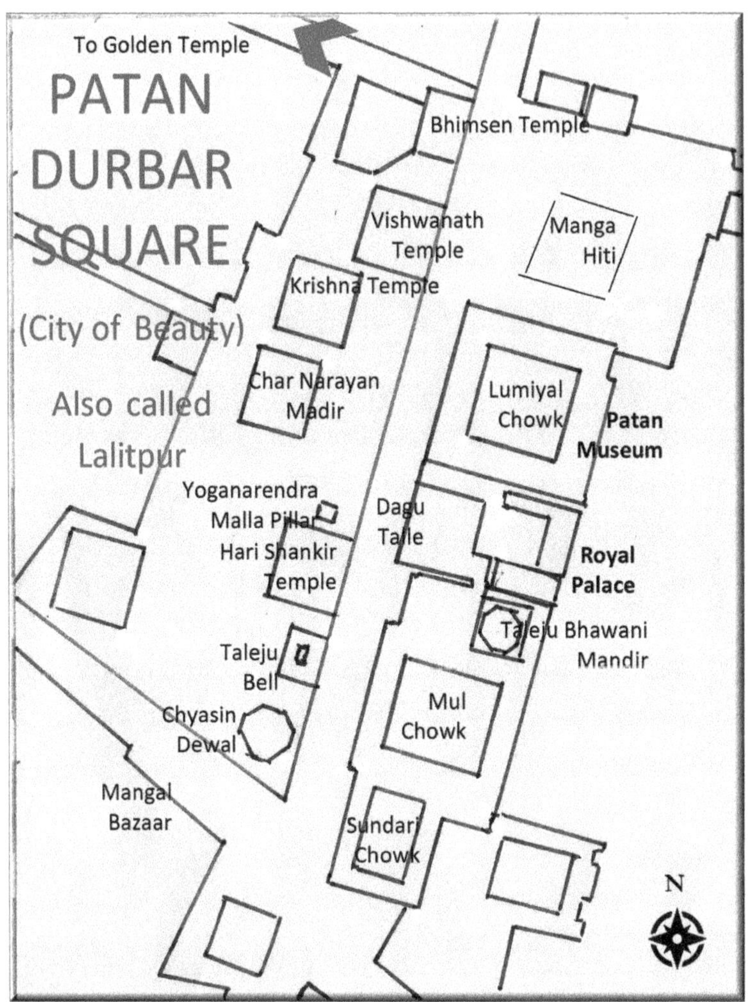

Map 8 – Patan or Lalitpur (City of Beauty) Durbar Square

Lumjyal Chowk
(Golden Window Courtyard)

Chyasin Dewal

He told his grieving subjects that, as long as the bird remained atop the cobra's head they would know he was still alive. For over a century, a bed was prepared for him nightly in the palace, in case he returned.

The two-tiered Char Narayan Mandir, built in 1565, is the oldest temple on the square, but largely ignored, although some of the scenes carved on the wooden struts are particularly interesting.

However, the Krishna Mandir, beside it, is most unusual with its central 'shikhara' spire surrounded by 3 levels of stone verandas displaying delicately carved friezes depicting scenes from the Mahabharata and Ramayana.

In front of the temple, atop another stone pillar kneels the gilt Garuda waiting to serve his master, Vishnu.

Bells and music are always heard from this temple as it is the most commonly used in this square. The Vishwanath Mandir, a 17th century pagoda, contains a copy of the Shiva linga of the same name in Varanasi, India.

Yoganendra Malla Statue

It collapsed without warning, in 1990, during the monsoon rains, but has been restored, although the massive stone elephants guarding the steps are a bit worse for the wear.

The road leading north from the square took us past some crumbling pagodas being restored until we reached the slender, five-storeyed temple of Khumbeshwar, Patan's oldest and tallest.

It was built as a two-tiered structure in 1392 with three upper roofs added in the 17th century and it still remains a well-proportioned and sturdy building.

Its name means 'Lord of the Water Pot' and the temple is considered the god's winter home.

The sacred water is said to be connected by underground channel with the pilgrimage site of Gosain Kund, the sacred lake high in the mountains north of Kathmandu.

This spring-fed water tank is the scene of the boisterous annual festival of Janai Purnima where Brahmins and Chhetris change their sacred threads (Janai) and worshippers lavish flowers, red powder and grains of rice on the embossed silver linga while crowds of young boys try to see how much water they can splash on the spectators.

Our last visit was to the three-tiered Hiranyavarna Mahabihara or 'Golden Temple', probably the most popular with tourists, and squeezed into the cramped courtyard of Kwa Bahal, a still active 12th century Buddhist Newar monastery and the spiritual hub of Old Patan.

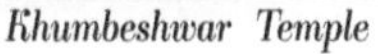

Khumbeshwar Temple

Golden Temple

The temple's brass facade is embossed with Buddhas and Taras, elephants, lions and snakes slithering off the second-storey roof.

Both the temple and the shrine are draped with patakas, supposed to provide a slide for the gods when they descend to answer the prayers of their worshippers.

We were required to remove our shoes before we entered which was a bit disconcerting as tortoises and rats were roaming the floor around the shrine. Buddha is the main image in the temple and the various alcoves around the courtyard.

The wealth on display is quite astounding and the maroon-clad monks and nuns continue the rhythm of their daily life just accepting the tourists as part of it. In days past, Newari merchants donated

Golden Temple (Note The patakas hanging down)

Golden Temple

portions of their profits for the temples' upkeep and I think wealthy donors must continue to sponsor it today. Prayer wheels rim the main courtyard while upstairs there is a large prayer wheel to turn among

Golden Temple

the chanting monks who insisted on sprinkling me with holy water. When we were there, a huge queue of worshippers waited to pray to the mother goddess for a wealth. Before we left Patan, we bought a couple of beautifully patterned brass dishes from the metalworkers.

After our evening meal we had to pack a smaller bag for our travels of the next 4 to 5 days – all very exciting.

Sunday 12th of April

After breakfast we left the hotel for Tribhuvan airport, once more, and an internal flight on Necon Airways to the town of Pokhara, at the foot of the Annapurna Range. The second largest city in Nepal, and situated 200 km west of the capital Kathmandu, Pokhara serves as the headquarters of the Kaski District. This green valley, dotted with half a dozen lakes, is lower and warmer than Kathmandu, its gentle climate nurturing all sorts of flowers.

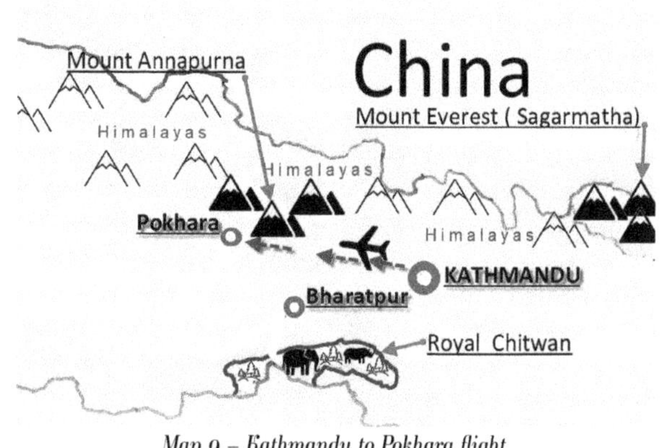

Map 9 – Kathmandu to Pokhara flight

This lush semitropical setting is backed by some of the highest peaks within 30 km of the town: Dhaulagiri, the Annapurna massif, Manaslu, Himalchuli and, though not so high, the soaring, twisting spire of Machhapuchhre, the world's 'Fishtail'.

Annapurna Range -view from Shangri-la Hotel – Machhapuchhre (Fishtail) to the right

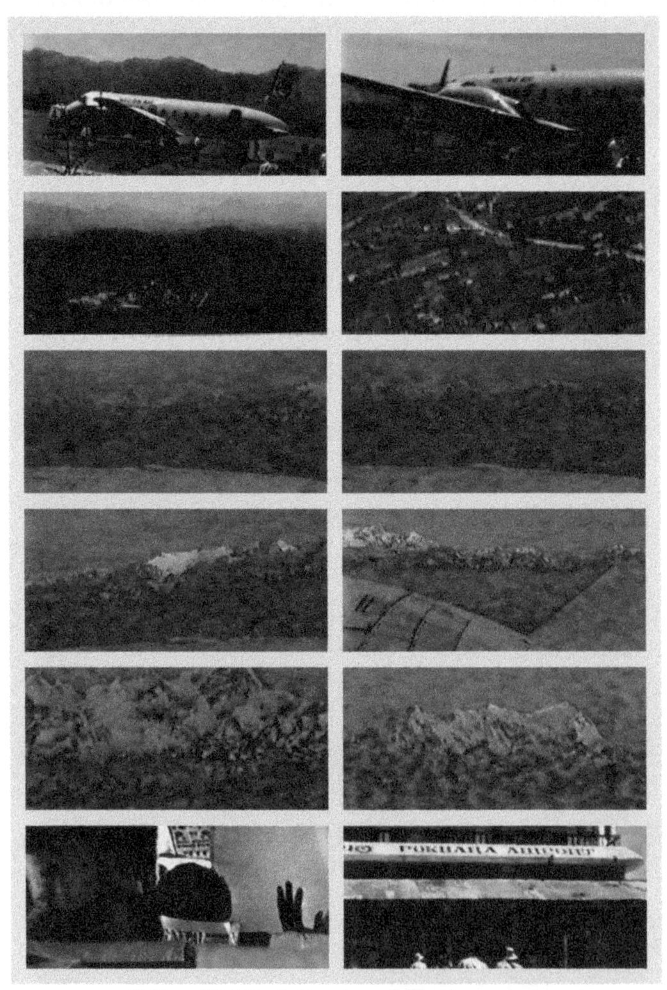

Pokhara Flight including views of The Annapurnas

The Seti-Gandaki (White River), is the main river flowing through the city and, along with its tributaries, it has created several gorges and canyons in and around the city.

The Seti Gorge itself runs through the whole city, north to south and west to east, and at places these gorges are only a few metres wide.

Dramatic Seti Gorge

In days gone by, Pokhara lay on the important trading route between China and India. In the 17th century, it was part of the kingdom of Kaski, one of the 24 kingdoms of Nepal, and ruled by a branch of the Shah dynasty.

Although Hindu castes now dominate the original Gurung inhabitants, many mediaeval ruins of large slate-roofed villages still dot the countryside. In 1786 Prithvi Narayan Shah added Pokhara to his kingdom and, as an important trading centre on route from Kathmandu to Jumla and India to Tibet, many Newars of Bhaktapur migrated to Pokhara on invitation by the king, and settled near the Bindhyabasini Temple.

The establishment of a British recruitment camp for Gurkha soldiers, however, brought many larger communities to Pokhara.

After the annexation of Tibet by China in 1962, the old trading route through Pokhara became defunct and today only a few caravans from Mustang arrive in Bagar. At this time, 300,000 exiles entered Nepal from neighbouring Tibet on their way to asylum communities in India.

Many decided to stay in Nepal because of their open religious tolerance and approximately 50 to 60,000 exiles reside here. 20,000 of them are in consolidated camps either in Kathmandu or in Pokhara.

The 4 Tibetan settlements in Pokhara are at Jampaling, Paljorling, Tashi Ling and Tashi Palkhiel. These are now well built settlements, each with a 'gompa', Buddhist monastery, 'chorten' (small stupas), schools and craft workshops making the Tibetans a visible minority in the area.

The municipality of Pokhara is quite loosely built up and still has much green space, and it is less claustrophobic, and appears cleaner than Kathmandu. Of course, until the end of the 1960s Pokhara was only accessible by foot and was, therefore, considered to be a more mystical place than Kathmandu.

Shangri-La Village Garden

The first 'road' was completed in 1968 (Siddhartha Highway) which we were to experience in a couple of days time. We were met at the airport, our luggage disappeared on a handcart, and we arrived at our lovely hotel of Shangri-La village.

Here we found lily ponds, reflecting pools, waterfalls and manicured lawns. Colonnaded walkways joined rooms, restaurants and coffee shops with small stupas and temples placed among an abundance of flowers. The views of the mountains were absolutely stunning.

Annapurna Range in the distance as viewed from the Hotel

Area surrounding the Shangri-La Village

Our young guide, Raji, met us at 3 pm for our first sojourn into Pokhara. Our first stop was at a point called Patale Chhango, popularly known as Devi's Falls.

Here the stream which overflows from Phewa Lake suddenly collapses and surges down the rocks into a deep gorge, leaping through several caves before taking a final plunge.

Seti Gorge -Devi Falls

The spot is, perhaps, more interesting as a source of popular mythology and has acquired its Western-sounding name from a female European, named Davis or Devin, who was drowned while skinny-dipping with her boyfriend.

The Nepalis have adopted the name Devi (which means goddess) and it is all perhaps a fabrication to warn the local youth to avoid promiscuous western ways.

Unfortunately, our guide told us that a young Nepali couple committed suicide there recently due to the difference in their castes not allowing them to marry.

The Seti gorge, as I said previously, carves a deep course through the city area and this can be viewed from various bridges.

We went to the Prithvi Highway bridge but, instead of the thundering turbulent river, it was only a small stream in the middle of a wide dry gravel area – the monsoon rains were due to fall in about 1-2 weeks and I'm sure this would change dramatically then.

The locals, however, were taking full advantage of the drought and, mainly women, were carrying huge sacks of sand and rocks from the riverbed, on their backs, and slowly walking up the hundreds of steps that led to the roadside where we stood.

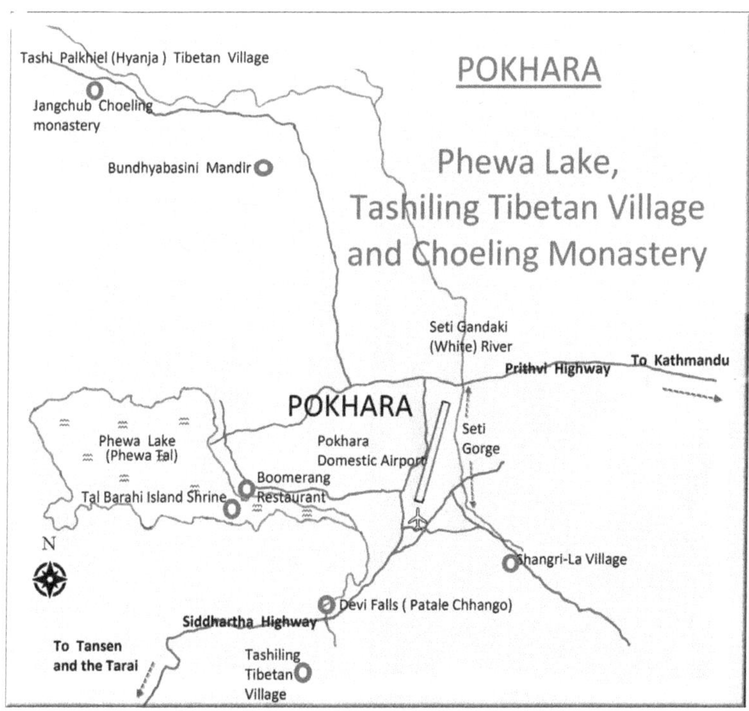

Map 10 Pokhara – Phewa Tal (Lake), Devi Falls, Tashiling Tibetan Village and Choeling

Machhapuchhre (Fishtail Mountain)

At the top more men and women were breaking the stones into smaller pieces using small metal hammers. This was the main material for the road building. As we walked to our next point of interest, Raji, indicated the many more modern concrete houses being built – these mainly belonged to the Ghorka people (Ghurkas).

Seti Gorge – Seti Gandaki (White) River

Comprising an elite corps within the British and Indian armies for over 175 years, the Gurkha regiments have been named amongst the finest fighting units of the world.

Ironically, the regiments were born out of the 1814-16 war between Nepal and the British East India Company and so impressed were the British by the men of "Goorkha " (Gorkha, the ancestral home of Nepal's rulers) that they began recruiting the Nepalis before the peace was even signed.

In the century that followed, Ghurkas fought in every major British military conflict, including two world wars, earning respect for their bravery.

Ghurkas mainly come from Mayar, Gurung, Rai and Limbu hill tribes and most boys from these groups dream of being accepted into the Ghurkas, not only for the money, but also for greater chance to see the world and return with prestige.

These modern and substantial homes, however, always tend to look unfinished as the Nepalis always leave the house with the possibility of adding another upper floor for the next generation.

Dictionary of The Nepali Language (1931)– 'The Ghurkas'

"As I write these last words, my thoughts return to you who were my comrades, the stubborn and indomitable peasants of Nepal. Once more I hear the laughter with which you greeted every hardship. Once more I see you in your bivouacs or about your fires, on forced march or in the trenches, now shivering with wet and cold, now scorched by a pitiless and burning sun. Uncomplaining you endure hunger and thirst

and wounds; and at the last your unwavering lines disappear into the smoke and wrath of battle. Bravest of the brave most generous of the generous, never had a country more faithful friends than you."

Sir Ralph Lilley Turner MC (5 October 1888 – 22 April 1983)

(Turner. Ralph L. 1931. A Comparative and Etymological Dictionary of the Nepali Language, London.)

Bundyhyabasini Mandir

On a hillock in the middle of this area is Bundhyabasini Mandir, a quiet temple complex, more noteworthy for its sweeping mountain views. The white shrines here are unremarkable architecturally (the originals having been destroyed by fire in 1949), but the temple is of great religious importance to Hindus living in the Pokhara region.

Buddhist Prayer Flags
Tibetans believe the prayers and mantras will be blown by the wind to spread good will and compassion.

The temple itself is dedicated to the goddess Durga, also known as Shakti or Kali, who is Pokhara's chosen guardian deity.

In Bundhyabasini she is seen as Bhagwatia, blood-thirsty aspect of the goddess, who is represented in the form of a 'shaligram', a spiral-shaped ammonite fossil or 'propitious stone' dating back 150 to 200 million years ago.

Animal sacrifices are, therefore, common here especially on Saturdays. In Nepal the sacrificing of animals such as chickens, pigeons, goats and even water buffaloes is commonly performed, an action completely alien to our sensibilities.

The blood is used to consecrate an image of the god or goddess being worshipped; an object which the worshipper asks that god to bless; or sometimes used as a tika to the worshippers.

Once the animal has been sacrificed, a portion, usually the head is presented to the god and the remainder is kept by the sacrificer usually for a feast.

Before the animal is sacrificed, the sacrificer will consult the animal and wait until it nods its head in acquiescence.

Those which take too long are sprinkled with water to get them to nod, but sometimes the sacrifice is delayed as a group follows the animal around waiting for its approval.

I must mention that only male animals are sacrificed – the one time it's good to be female.

Back then through Pokhara centre and past many paddyfields fed by rows of small canals filled with mountain water, to our hotel for dinner at the Caravanserai restaurant – an Indian buffet tonight, with entertainment.

Walking back to our room we noticed Halley's Comet quite clearly in the starlit sky, in a completely different position from where we saw it in our sky at home.

Monday, 13th of April

When the birdsong awoke us in the morning and we drew back the curtains the scene before us was absolutely stunning, snowy Machhapuchhre (Fish Tail Mountain) was resplendent against the blue sky.

The flowers were beautiful and we could see the oxen or water buffalo ploughing the nearby fields.

The beautiful Annapurna peaks – viewed in sunlight from the Hotel

Women were out already planting in the paddyfields and two men were thatching a roof in the compound of the hotel. Another beautiful day!

A stunning Annapurna sunrise

Pokhara, Nepal's second largest City

Buses being washed in a riverbed

Nepali painting showing the double-finned summit of Machhapuchhre – "Fishtail"

Today we were to head north of Pokhara to begin with, cross the Seti river, and visit Tashi Palkhiel (Hyanja) one of the Tibetan villages situated around the town.

Jangchub Choeling Monastery
Entrance Tashi Palkhiel (Hyanja) – Tibetan Village

On the way, the first sight that amused us was the view of the buses and trucks in the middle of the river having their daily wash.

When the Chinese invaded Tibet in 1950, and the Dalai Lama fled in 1959, the Tibetans now living in Pokhara were mostly peasants and nomads living in the border areas of western Tibet.

The political changes in Lhasa left them unaffected initially, but when the Chinese occupation turned more autocratic thousands poured south through the Himalaya to safety.

They gathered further north to begin with and then, when conditions became desperate, the Swiss Red Cross relocated 2000 refugees to 3 transit camps around Pokhara.

The first five years were hard with food rationing, chronic sickness and general unemployment. However, with the construction of the Pardi Dam and the Prithvi and Siddhartha highways much work was provided.

Because Pokhara, unlike Kathmandu, has no holy Buddhist places, most Tibetans have remained in camps where they have built their 'gompas' (monasteries), weaving halls, schools where English is taught, old people's homes, clinics and community halls.

Interior view of Jangchub Choeling Monastery

Nepal can truly say it is the home of Buddhism as Siddartha Gautama, who became the Buddha, was born in present-day Nepal in Lumbini in the Terai, about 563 BC.

A Further Interior view of Jangchub Choeling Monastery

Buddhist Prayer Flags

Today Nepal is one of the great centres of Tibetan Buddhism across the northern Himalayan region.

After the death of Siddartha Gautama about 480 BC Buddhism grew quickly and when Ashoka, the first great emperor of India, converted to Buddhism in 263BC it grew even greater.

He is supposedly said to have visited Patan and built 4 large stupas to mark the cardinal points. Symbols of the people's faith fill the hillsides and villages.

Strings of thin cotton flags flap in the breezes, each printed with a Buddhist prayer sent to heaven in the wind.

"Mane" wheels are cylinders with a mantra or prayer placed inside and which also depend on constant motion to carry the prayers to heaven.

Some are set along walls or in temples and, as people walk by, they give the wheel a spin earning merit for themselves or the person who installed the wheels.

Smaller 'mane' wheels are carried by the elderly, mostly, and a flick of the wrist keeps the wheel spinning as they go about their daily business.

We were walking to the Jangchub Choeling Monastery, begun in 1963 by Lama Dupseng Rinpoche. Over time, the number of devotees grew and parents began to ask the Lama to ordain their sons as monks.

Over the last 20 to 30 years Shangpa Rinpoche has continually expanded and improved the 'facilities'.

The present shrine hall was built in 1991 and an educational institute with new and larger dormitory rooms had just been completed.

The architecture of the shrine hall is true to traditional Tibetan design with the main hall being dominated by a 7 feet copper and gold-plated statue of Buddha. On the back wall are 1000 small Buddha figures representing the 1000 Buddhas believed to exist in this ' Fortunate Era'.

Using traffic to separate the grain seeds from the husks on the road to Begnas Tal

The wall paintings by the Tibetan artist Mr Dhawa, portray the life of Buddha while facing the Buddha are portraits of the 16 Arhats who upheld Buddha's teachings. We had the shrine to ourselves, but on emerging to retrieve our shoes we were met by the strident blowing of horns and hundreds of people appearing from within a large hall.

Apparently a special lama (a spiritual teacher) was visiting the community and had been giving a sermon to all the villagers. It was

Tashi Palkhel (Hyangia) Tibetan Settlement =Jangchub Choeling Monastery

a noisy and colourful scene as all the young monks, complete with personal stereos and American sneakers, leapt around joyfully.

The Tibetan woven aprons and hats were very eye-catching with their beads and mane wheels and everyone appeared to be in a good state of health and prosperity – in complete contrast to Kathmandu.

Our next port of call involved travelling over an extremely bumpy road to the twin lakes of Begnas Tal and Rupa Tal set in astounding countryside.

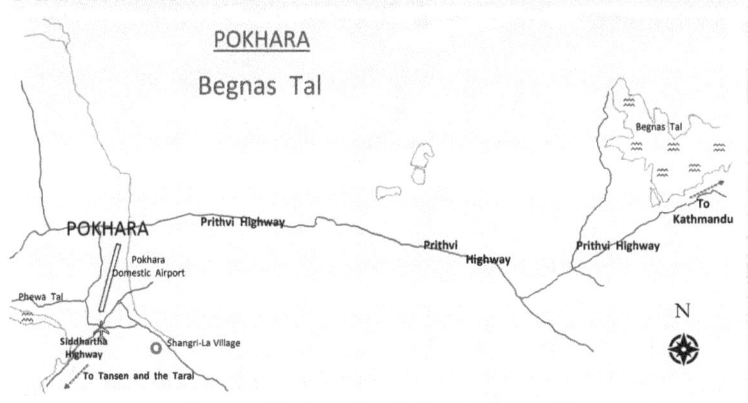

Map 11 – The Road From Pokhara to Begnas Tal

Road To Begnas Tal, Dam and Lake

Begnas Tal, the bigger lake, is framed by meticulously engineered paddy terraces, marching right down to its shore, while Rupa Tal on the other side of the intervening ridge remains practically hidden.

Below the dam at the south end, the Ministry of Agriculture has built a huge fish farm filled with carp and trout. Small boats line the shore, and when we were there some were being repaired and painted.

Begnas Tal

It was quite an idyllic spot with only a few families picnicking on the grassy bank.

Of course, the ubiquitous goats and their kids were there and drew much attention. Apparently Prince Charles had camped on the other side of the lake only the previous Friday.

A leisurely walk back to the road and we were off to Phewa Tal and the Boomerang restaurant for a quick pizza. The centre piece of Pokhara is this beautiful lake with lodges and restaurants stretched along the eastern shore.

Phewa Tal, Pokhara

According to legend it was once a prosperous valley whose people one day scorned a wandering beggar. Finding one sympathetic woman he warned her of an impending flood.

She duly fled with her family to higher ground while a torrent roared down from the mountains and submerged the town – the

Phewa Tal, Pokhara with the island shrine Tal Barahi central in the distance

Approaching the Island Shrine Tal Barahi on Phewa Tal, by boat

Phewa Tal

'beggar' being none other than the goddess Barahi Bhagwati.

The woman's descendants settled beside the new lake and erected the island shrine of the Tal Barahi.

The geological explanation is that the entire Pokhara Valley was submerged, just like Kathmandu. Over time the Seti river eroded an ever growing outlet lowering the water level and leaving Phewa Tal and several smaller lakes as remnants.

The lake has enlarged in the recent past probably due to a blocked outlet (perhaps during an earthquake) and, of course, the installation of the Pardi Hydroelectric Dam has increased the lake size and there are fears of silting up due to the inflow of floodwater during monsoon.

We climbed into a small boat and were paddled across to the island shrine of Tal Barahi. Whilst the temple is reasonably modern, it is often busy at weekends, when the lake goddess exacts a steady tribute of blood sacrifices.

A ring of the bell and a walk around to admire the scenery and also the King's summer residence, only a few hundred metres from the island on shore, was all we had time for. Lots of people were swimming, but we were told the water was very polluted – best not to fall in then! Our journey back was a bit more wobbly – I think our paddler was in a hurry but we did catch sight of a few egrets and kingfishers.

Hotel Colonnade

Raji took us back to the Tashiling Buddhist settlement, this time however, to have the opportunity to purchase some souvenirs.

On return to the hotel he presented us with woven bracelets – a good luck charm for tomorrow – their New Year's Day, 2055. A good meal, packing once again and the advent of a huge spider on the bedroom wall was all I had to report.

Tuesday 14th April

The only through road beyond Pokhara is the Siddhartha Highway which gives you a slow, uncomfortable ride to the Terai. The 160 km road crosses four major rivers, negotiates countless twists and turns and often claims a tyre or an axle. The driver arrived early with an old Toyota vehicle, and almost bald tyres – Graham immediately wondered if we would reach the jungle in this vehicle.

It was a very hot day but it was impossible to open the windows because of the clouds of road dust. No such thing as air-con in this vehicle. Some sections of the road were tarmac but the majority was still unmade. All the way we came across groups of men rebuilding small sections of the road and, I have to say, skillfully, using basic raw materials and equipment to achieve this – perhaps one day all these newer short sections will be joined up.

We saw huge piles of large rocks dotted along the highway, sometimes even spilling onto the roadway. Then there were groups of workers painstakingly breaking the rocks into small pieces with a hammer. Nearby a large rectangular rusty metal pan was sitting over a small fire melting the road tar.

It all seemed efficient enough but a very slow process. We must have passed at least a dozens of these road surface construction working parties each with their overnight tent accommodation alongside.

From Pokhara, the road initially labours 800m up to a high point before descending to Naudanda, a small village with houses set high and perilously close to the river's edge.

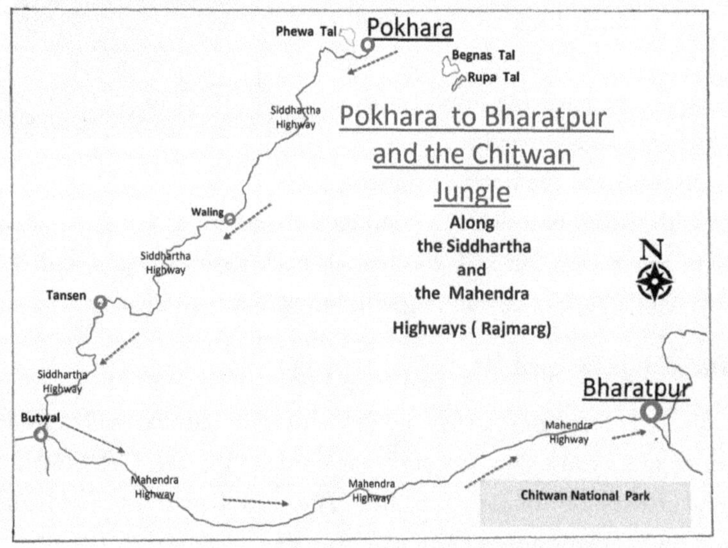

Map 12 -Pokhara to Bharatpur and the Chitwan Jungle along the Siddhartha Highway and the Mahendra Highway

Siddhartha Highway Traffic

We had to remember that this was New Year's Day but daily life was continuing as normal: buffalo ploughing; paddy fields being planted and even a unique form of corn threshing.

This was undertaken by the women who laid the sheaves of corn across this main traffic thoroughfare, waiting for the tyres of the traffic to crush them.

Traffic, we noticed, was steady, but only comprising large gaudily painted trucks and buses jam-packed with passengers – not a car in sight. In addition, motorbikes and bicycles were popular nearer the villages but

Highway Construction

Mule Train on the Siddhartha Highway

mostly people were walking and carrying huge bundles on their backs. There were several bridges to cross over some very deep gorges too. Many of the bridges were still wooden, and it was unnerving when our driver touched all the gods and goddesses sitting on his dashboard and also repeated a small prayer before crossing each one.

One bridge required a toll payment before crossing even for individual goats and donkeys with only a single vehicle being permitted to cross over at any one time.

Entering the Amdi Khola watershed, the highway wriggled tortuously across the side of the valley and, at times, we would suddenly be faced, usually on a blind corner, by a mule train – a very long line of laden, tinkling animals, anything up to 50 mules long.

This used to be the only form of transport on the old trade route – in most cases they would emerge out of a cloud of dust. Of course, there were lots of other animals on the road – goats, cows, water buffaloes, and chickens – and our driver never slowed down once, but rather pressed the horn almost continuously.

We had one stop for the toilet a hut, with no door and a pail of water for flushing / washing purposes – very perfunctory. After the town of Syangia, hills began to rear up spectacularly as the valley narrowed and it was not long before we crossed the rugged canyon of Kali Gandaki where we could look down and see river rafting, although the river beds were almost dry.

Climbing then to about 1000m, the road has about an hour's descent to the town of Butwal and the Terai.

Scenery, including rice paddy fields, along the Siddhartha Highway

The last 40 km stretch is apparently prone to landslides and was in a dreadful state, especially as our driver swerved to avoid loose rocks and often veered towards sheer, unprotected cliff edges.

Suddenly we were in woodland and then more lush tropical vegetation as we followed the Trisuli River and after our 5½ to 6 hr journey we arrived dusty and battered but safe in Butwal. Here we said our goodbyes to the driver and were transferred to a jeep for the next part of the journey.

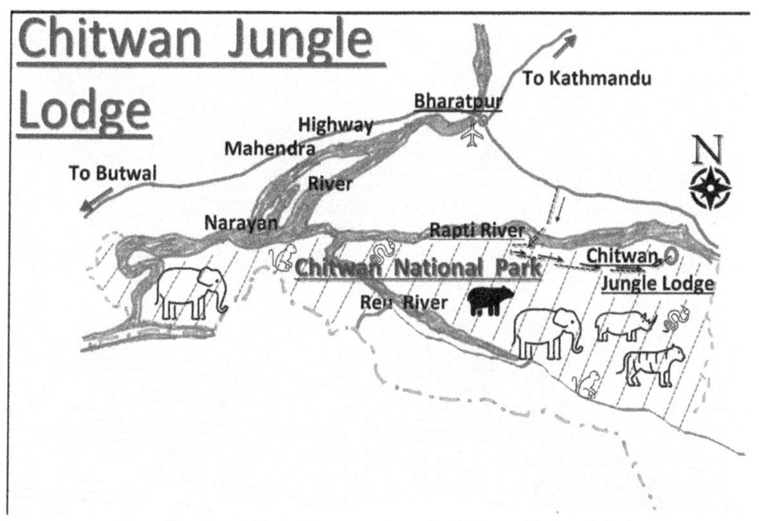

Map 13 – Route From Bharatpur into the Chitwan National Park

Our first stop was the local airport (a loose term) at Bharatpur to reconfirm our tickets back to Kathmandu with Royal Nepal Airlines. The airport is just a field where a siren sounds to clear the locals when an aeroplane lands.

The airport terminal is a stone structure about 20' x 10' with a few broken plastic seats – no doors, no windows, just openings – and a set of scales carried from a shop nearby to weigh the luggage as and when flights arrive.

Not far from here, we changed vehicles once more and were put in an open-top jeep while our luggage disappeared elsewhere.

Two guides in army camouflage now drove us to the Chitwan Jungle. Once we had left the Mahendra Highway – the only road running east and west – we drove on narrow tracks and then into and across the Rapti River, with the water rising pretty close to where we were sitting- all unexpected and very exciting.

A change of vehicle to ford the Rapti River and onwards through the jungle

We continued on past Tharu tribe villages with lots of barefoot children and barking dogs and then up to the outer jungle perimeter to an army post, where we had to wait for clearance. The army role is to protect the National Park from poachers.

We knew we were in the jungle now as the track narrowed further and was enclosed by trees. The driver now slowed down and became more alert when suddenly we saw a huge elephant carrying a full load of branches bounding along the road in front of us. I was quite unaware as to how quickly these animals can move.

Animal outlines in the jungle

Soon we arrived at the Chitwan Jungle Lodge, our home for the next few days. The Terai is the northern limit of the enormous flood-plain of the River Ganges, the great holy river of the Hindu religion, and this area is greatly influenced by Indian customs and culture.

The Terai is a belt of marshy grasslands, savannas, and forests, located south of the outer foothills of the Himalaya and includes the Royal Chitwan National Park which was established in 1973 and is full of wildlife as well as rich flora and fauna. Chitwan means both 'heart of the jungle' or 'leopard forest'. In 1976 the park was enlarged to 1,040 square miles, its current size.

Chitwan is actually only 150m above sea level and can get steamy from March-June, with peak temperatures reaching 43°C in the shade. The monsoon season (July-August) is intense, with pounding rain, swollen rivers, luxuriant vegetation and high humidity and insects.

The flat low altitude is in complete contrast to the national image of mountains, and it covers less than $^1/_5$ of the total area of the country. Until the 1950s, a journey through the Terai was a quick rush through the jungle, trying to avoid tigers, rhinos, elephants, cobras and other poisonous snakes and scorpions.

Priorities never change

Most feared, of course, was the thick, buzzing clouds of mosquitoes carrying a particularly severe strain of malaria called the dreaded 'aul'. Traditionally, the government of Nepal only granted lands in the Terai to high generals and officials who behaved like feudal lords giving a share of their harvest to the King.

Equally, the Rana dynasty desired the continued isolation of Nepal from outside influence and they considered the jungle their private hunting ground. In 1938-39 a hunt to entertain the Viceroy of India, included killing 120 tigers, 38 rhinos, 27 leopards and 15 bears at one fell swoop. Development of agriculture and timber felling developed slowly although it was realised that the fertile soil had great economic potential.

Only when the World Health Organisation sprayed the area with DDT in an attempt to control the mosquitoes, did the countryside open. Today, it is one of the fastest growing areas and now is the 'bread basket' and 'rice bowl' of the nation producing 60% of grain and containing 50% of the population. Apart from the arable land, most of the region is covered in tropical, deciduous forest, the last remnants of prehistoric times. Lush grasslands and fine hardwood 'sal' trees have always harboured a dense and diverse wildlife population.

One- Horned Rhino

Although much of the forest has been levelled for agricultural purposes, the government set aside sizeable chunks for national parks and reserves. In 1973 the Chitwan National Park was formed to protect dwindling numbers of endangered species.

The dense forests here provide cover for predators such as tigers and leopards; the swampy grassland, a great habitat for rhinoceros and many species of deer; and the rivers for two types of crocodile and dolphins. The seesaw battle for survival of Chitwan continues and, although they have based an army battalion in the park to prevent poaching, the practice still continues.

When we were there, the last count showed 100 tigers and 51 different mammalian species living in the forest, including an illusive herd of wild elephants which can cause great destruction. On our arrival we were taken to our hut which was of a bamboo construction with thatched roof and mesh windows. Apart from the two beds, there was a toilet and cold shower that didn't work, but no mosquito nets.

We were told that there were only two hours of electricity a day – between 6:00pm and 8:00pm – and that we would have kerosene lamps otherwise, which were required to be placed outside the door at night, to keep the animals away.

The small gardens around the lodges were filled with beautiful flowers and it was possible to wander around and admire the bougainvillea and orchids and the colourful birds flying around.

However it was strictly forbidden to step outside the central area because of the danger. There were no fences, so the animals could wander in if they wished.

We had lunch at 1:00 pm – it was some kind of very tough buffalo meat – and then we were treated to a lecture on Asian elephants, animals we would come to know quite well over thenext couple of days. Asian elephants have been ceremonial beasts of burden for thousands of years and have survived, mainly as domesticated animals.

Jungle Lodge Communal Area

With a brain four times the size of a human, they are thought to be as intelligent as dolphins. Although they appear docile, they all have strong individual personalities and moods. They learn dozens of commands but, as any mahout (the keeper and driver of an elephant) will tell you, they only obey one handler and then, only if they want to.

Their average daily intake is 200 litres of water and 250 kg of foods which consists of concentrated rations of molasses, salt and grain all wrapped in a football sized bundle of grass. Of course, like many animals, they graze all the time, grasping wisps of elephant grass as they amble along. The trunk contains 40,000 muscles and apart from eating and drinking, can lift a man with little effort. They usually live for 70 to 80 years.

At 4:30 pm a bell rang and this was the call for our first activity. We were to go for a jungle drive in an open-topped Jeep. Although there are many creatures in the jungle, the dense vegetation doesn't allow for easy sightings, and often people are disappointed in this respect – you need to be very alert and look for the slightest movement.

Firstly we saw something moving in the grass, but it was almost impossible to discern what it was but possibly a leopard – this was confirmed later. We saw 4 different species of deer: sambar, spotted, barking and hog and many of the hundreds species of birds, although they were difficult to identify whilst moving.

Then suddenly I spotted something which sent a shiver down my spine. "Big black snake" I shouted out and we just caught its tail disappearing into the foliage. It was long – thicker than an arm and black all over.

The guides were very interested and marked that area on their map as a part to be avoided. This was the King Cobra, the most dangerous snake in that area, which can kill an elephant in 15 minutes.

Beautiful bougainvllea in the garden of the compound - an area beyond which we were not allowed to go unescorted

As darkness was falling, we returned to the camp and, at 6:30 pm, we were given a talk and shown examples of all the poisonous snakes and deadly spiders and informed on the tigers, rhinos, gaurs (Indian bison) and the extremely dangerous sloth bears.

While we were sitting there, in pitch darkness, a small furry kitten jumped up on my knee – I must have jumped a foot in the air.

Views of the Chitwan National Park

A barbecue-style dinner was later served outside in lamplight and then a crowd of Tharu villagers ran barefoot into the camp.

The Tharu are the only indigenous people of this region and they are a handsome, gentle people who have a natural immunity to the malaria and make their living by farming small settlements – not without its dangers, on the edge of the jungle.

A display of the Tharu Stick Dance ensued, as a mock battle took place with extremely graceful movement and split second timing – it was very noisy. Apparently, the original purpose of the dance was to make a lot of noise and keep the wild animals away.

Soon after the performance we groped our way to bed with our kerosene lamp. Mosquitoes were everywhere, both in and out, and so

The Tharu Stick Dance

I wrapped myself in the bed sheet and tried to sleep.

The noise, as in all jungles, was incredible:

- the ceaseless chirping of the cicadas;
- the croaks of the frogs;

After dark in the Jungle Lodge area

- the piercing call of the jungle cuckoo (' just one more bottle')
- the screeches of the monkeys and birds and
- the drumming and singing of the Tharu tribesmen.

All this made me very restless for about an hour.

Then suddenly, as the tribesmen's drums faded into the distance, the jungle went eerily silent. I thought that it can't be morning and this was so very strange, when suddenly, outside our window, I heard this blood-curdling snarl and growl. Graham thought I had imagined it all, but, along with the guide next day we saw a tiger print in the sand outside our window.

Wednesday 15th April

Awakened at 5:00 am, we assembled for coffee and tea at 5:30 am ready for our next adventure – an elephant ride. Once we had climbed on the elephant's back, in a most ungainly manner, we set off at a stately gait and, once we got used to the gentle rocking movement, we could imagine that we were part of a foreign delegation entering Nepal for the first time.

The mahout (driver) sat astride the elephant's head giving commands using his toes to press behind its ears and an occasional whack on the head with a small stick. On this ride we were at the complete mercy of the terrain:

- falling backwards going up the hills or steep riverbanks
- thrown forwards when descending
- splashed with water when travelling through the rivers
- and hit with rebounding high grasses or branches all covered in spiders' webs and insects.

The rivers at this time of year, just before the monsoon rains, were almost dry and so it was a good place to spot animals in search of a drink. I think we were too late, however, as we saw tiger prints, deer hoof marks, and long python trails on the sand, but only a few birds and deer in the grassland.

The Indian elephant

The Chitwan National Park – views of the Nepali Terai

It did not matter, however, as it was a beautiful morning and the sun shining on the distant ice-clad mountains was magnificent.

Returning to camp by 8:00am, we had a leisurely breakfast before our 10:00am Jungle Walk. This is a wonderful way to experience the reserve, so long as all goes well. We set off through peaceful woods, shuffling our feet through layers of dead leaves.

There were lots of birds around: parakeets, paradise flycatchers, kingfishers, hornbills and ospreys. Sometimes we saw langur monkeys swinging from the trees and our guides pointed out orchids, strangler figs, termite mounds, tiger prints, rhino droppings and snake trails – all very exciting, but I am sure everyone was thinking 'what if we stand on a snake?' or, 'what if we meet a rhino or tiger or even a sloth bear?' – all are possible and all that our guides had for our protection were a couple of sticks.

Very interesting early morning jungle walk -just don't stand on the snakes

Staying alive here is a serious issue and the younger guides tend to play down the risks. 100 people have been killed by rhino since records began in 1979 and 20 by tigers, although they have been locals mostly. However, 2 to 3 tourist maulings a year take place.

Our guides joked about an American who disobeyed the rules and went walkabout alone and got lost. He was attacked by a sloth bear, but luckily made it back with only a few scratches and the loss of his watch. The joke is that every time the guides spot a sloth bear they check to see if it is wearing a watch.

There are no emergency medical facilities nearby and the closest hospital is at Bharatpur, about two hours away, and so if anyone has a major bleed bad luck! It is imperative not to enter the jungle without a guide, but even then, in an emergency situation, he can only tend to one person at a time, so you are really responsible for your own safety.

We were told that if a rhino charges, run in a zig- zag path, throw off a piece of clothing and climb the nearest tree – easier said than done!

We saw more tiger paw prints near the river and climbed a high look-out tower to admire the view. As we were halfway climbing up our guide added "Oh bears sometimes sleep up there!". By the time we returned to camp for lunch the temperature was a steamy 36°- rather hot.

At 3:30 pm the elephants had a bath in the river and much hilarity was had by all – especially those who climbed on their backs and were drenched by their trunk hosepipe actions.

An amazing animal close-up

Elephants enjoying river bathing

Great fun in the river and a well earned rest

One-horned rhinos out and about

Mother rhino and baby enjoying a mud pool

By 4:30pm we were back on our elephant, for our grasslands Jungle Safari – this time facing the rear.

Heading on a different route through the tall grass we did feel that this was the best and safest way to spot wild life. We were lucky on this trip and saw one large rhino and also, wonderfully, a rhino mother and baby in a wallow having a mud bath.

Rhinos have terrible eyesight, but keen senses of smell and hearing.

Fortunately, the scent of the elephant masks a human smell, enabling us to go very close and view these prehistoric tanks with their armour-plated skin, twitching ears and highly coveted horns.

Asian 'gaida'- one horned rhinos – weigh 2 tonnes, have no sweat glands and spend much time wallowing in rivers to coat their hides in mud as protection from the sun and insects.

They are vegetarians and tend to be solitary and suspicious, although surprisingly agile creatures, whose small brain makes them unpredictable and illogical and prone to blind charges.

Their weak point is their horn made of compressed dermal fibres and whose purpose is unknown as they mainly use tusks for defence.

Unfortunately, this latter item is greatly sought after for use in Chinese medicine. The locals have many customs, too, and keep rhino skin bracelets to protect against evil spirits, rhino dung as a laxative and rhino urine to cure tuberculosis.

The Royal Bengal Tiger (Bagh), on the other hand is a secret and reclusive creature and can only be detected by a paw print or occasional roar.

We did not come across a tiger although we saw many prints but on our way back to camp in the dusk, I am sure I saw one sitting in the foliage in the distance watching us – I believe it, anyway!

We did see 3 sloth bears as the dark was falling. Firstly, a mother and baby at the foot of a termite mound. Our mahout kept saying "Very dangerous", "Very dangerous", but continued to go closer and closer.

We had been warned that these bears would easily jump on and attack an elephant with their fiercely curved claws.

And hidden amongst the tree...

Dusk settling on the Chitwan

Only when we spotted the father standing on his hind legs did we about turn and head back.

Graham had developed quite severe tummy problems this evening so we missed the farewell dinner and retired early.

Our Jungle – Airport Transfer

Thursday 16th April

Due to Graham's illness the previous night we did not attend the early morning bird watching but remained in bed for some extra rest. I attended breakfast alone and packed up our belongings.

We waved farewell to our jungle home of swarming ants and mosquitoes and travelled in a landrover to the nearby army post. Here we transferred to a military truck which bounced along the

Bharatpur Domestic Airport Terminal

rough, uneven tracks at a remarkable speed with only the Tharu children and barking dogs rushing to wave us goodbye.

Back to civilisation and the Mahendra Highway, we headed west for Bharatpur Airport.

Our flight was delayed for 2 hours — we knew not why! And so we sat sweltering on the broken plastic seats in unending heat with our luke-warm bottles of water. Eventually, the small battered plane arrived and disgorged half a dozen passengers.

Believe it or not our luggage was thoroughly searched outside on the grass and then we were personally searched in the toilets.

This old, non- pressurised rust bucket had 20 seats and even holes in the door. The air stewardess, who sat in the back seat, handed out sweets and cotton wool for our ears, smiling bravely.

What a flight! We took off on a grass runway and then bounced along in the air at a low altitude just skimming mountains and hitting frequent air pockets for about 1½ hours – I was so sick, as were many others.

Arriving in Kathmandu feeling pretty wobbly Rajesh, our organiser, took us back to the hotel with care and comforting words. We both went straight to bed and slept for a few hours.

A quite surreal situation arose at this point. I heard bagpipes playing 'Over the sea to Skye', and wondered if it was part of a dream, but on reaching consciousness and pulling back the curtains, I discovered a Ghurka pipe band playing in the garden.

This was a reception for the Danish Embassy personnel which was being held by the hotel owner (a royal princess).

What better to do than go down and join them as we were feeling much revived. A Nepalese meal with music followed as well as much catching up, with new friends.

Friday 17th of April

Nestling amid the valley's best farmland, today we were to visit Bhaktapur or 'Bhadgaon' the 'City of Devotees'.

"Were there nothing else in Nepal, save the Durbar Square of Bhatgaon (Bhaktapur), it would still be amply worth making a journey halfway around the globe to see."

E.A. Powell *(The Last Home Of Mystery, 1929, London.)*

Perhaps, because it lay off the main India – Tibet route this conch-shaped city, which began as a series of villages, has preserved its mediaeval ambience, elegant art, and colourful festivals of the Newari lifestyle. Hinduism has hardly been diluted by Buddhism, here, and westernisation has been very slow to take root.

Percival Landon, the early twentieth – century traveller, wrote that Bhaktapur was Nepal's 'most perfectly preserved city' with bricks everywhere – the streets and the houses and temples.

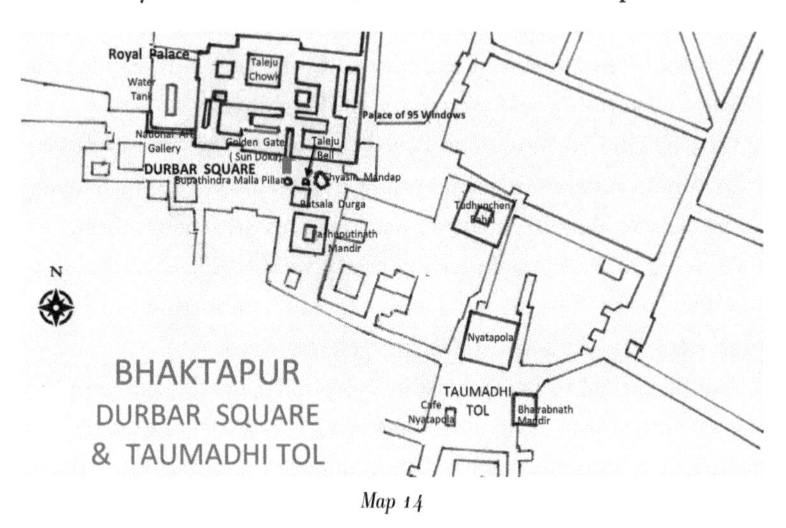

Map 14

In spite of constant invasions and natural calamities, especially the 1934 earthquake, much has been renovated and still boasts the art and culture of bygone eras.

Probably founded in the 9th century, it rose to rule Nepal by 1200 A.D. when King Arideva bestowed the title Malla, (Wrestler), on his son – today carved wrestlers are the city's trademark temple guardians.

When Yaksha Malla divided the kingdom between his three sons the squabbling lasted for years but it was the King of Bhaktapur who brought the Malla era to a close in 1766 by inviting Prithvi Narayan Shah, the Ghorka leader, to help him in a quarrel with Kathmandu. As a result the Valley was conquered within three years, Bhaktapur being the last to surrender.

A town of artists and craftsmen, the narrow alleys and twisted lanes are usually filled with potters, metalworkers and carvers, but today was the rowdy Bisket Jatra festival and the streets and squares were filled with many bands made up of drums and flutes, singing and dancing.

One of the many bands marching round the city and all playing different tunes

Bisket Jatra is celebrated in mid-April at the beginning of the Nepalese New Year when the god Bhairab, and his spouse Bhadrakala, are hauled in chariots through the streets.

Everyone was dressed in their finery: the men with their hats and waistcoats as they dragged the goats to sacrifice; the Newari women wearing the traditional black and red trimmed 'pataasi', wrapped around their waist in tiers, giving the effect of a flamenco skirt and showing their tattooed ankles which allows them entrance to heaven; and the many wonderful Indian saris as the women queued with baskets of food to do 'puja' at the temples and shrines.

This is a city with lots of public space, where each caste-based neighbourhood has its own square, own water source and own temples. The brick-paved main artery, however, winds its way unmarred by traffic through 3 main squares lined with richly decorated temples and shrines and all connected by quaint little streets.

Another festival band

It was all very colourful and exciting today, seeing everyone enjoying themselves (some a little too much), so it was difficult to concentrate on the buildings themselves.

Durbar Square in Bhaktapur used to be one of the most beautiful squares of all the kingdoms, but the 1934 earthquake devastated a number of the temples leaving odd blank spaces and consequently destroying it as a social focal point – but not today, as crowds queued for the temples and bands passed through one after another.

It is still imposing, however, and in 1994 it had a brief, but magnificent renaissance when it was used for ancient flashback scenes in the film "Little Buddha". Despite all this, it boasts one of Nepal's proudest artistic achievements, the 'Golden Gate'-

"the most exquisitely designed and finished piece of gilded metalwork in all Asia".

It is, in fact, made of brass, but its detail raises it to the level of a masterpiece. The 'torana' above the door features a squat Garud and a ten-armed, four – headed Taleju, the Mallas guardian deity.

To the locals, the most powerful figures are those of Bhairab and Kali, on either side of the gate. This is the entry to the once Royal Palace which, at one time, had 90 courtyards.

The present structure dates from the 18th century and is greatly scaled down, but with a superbly carved eastern wing 'The Palace of the 55 Windows", being the main attraction.

Bupathindra Malla, Bhaktapur's builder King kneels atop a pillar facing the building with his hands folded in prayer or respect. Historical chronicles state that the king placed a single pane of glass carried from India into one of the windows as an 'object of wonder' for the people.

Inside, and through another old doorway, we could view Bupathindra's old Royal Bath once filled with water by a gilded metal spout and guarded by a gilded 'nag' figure.

Once a centrepiece of the palace, lit by oil lamps for the Royal ablutions it is now overgrown with ferns and is a sad reflection of a now, obliterated, palace.

Hidden around the corner is the sacred temple of Taleju, but it is closed to non-Hindus and we had to be content with peering through the guarded doorway at the richly carved and ornamented courtyard.

In the whole square, the only surviving temple which commands respect is the Pashupatinath Mandir, a replica of the original, minus the gilt roof and silver doors. Originally the oldest structure, it houses a copy of the exalted "linga" and some very erotic carvings.

The Golden Gate (Background) and the Bell of The Taleju Bell (To the right)

Nearby stands the stone 'shikhara' of Batsala Durga complete with large Taleju Bell plus a smaller version generally known as the 'Bell of the Barking Dogs' as its toll apparently inflicts ultrasonic pain on the local hounds.

Behind the bell, the eight sided Chyasalin Mandap, the "Pavilion of Eight Corners" was originally a viewpoint for nobles to observe festivals and rituals.

Destroyed in the 1934 earthquake, it was lovingly rebuilt by local workmen fitting together the new woodcarving with the old and rubbing it all over with linseed oil to achieve uniformity.

At the far west corner, near the main gate we saw two multi armed statues of Bhairab and Ugrachandi, whose sculptor rather gruesomely had his hands cut off so that he couldn't reproduce similar images in Kathmandu or Patan.

Over at the south-eastern corner of the Royal Palace stands the 17th Century stone Siddhi Lakshmi Temple also known as the Lohan Dega or Stone Temple.

The steps are flanked by male and female attendants each leading a reluctant child and an eager-looking dog. On successive levels are horses, rhinos, man-lions and camels.

Making our way north east now, we came on an enormous plaza littered with the bases of giant temples – all destroyed – although closeby was the well preserved Tadhunchem Bahal, which attracts Buddhists as well as Hindus.

Following the winding brick road east through the city's main artery, we passed tiny shops selling sweets, cloth, carvings and brass.

Further on we reached wells and ancient water tanks where women struggled to do the daily washing, celebrations or not and then down a rather odorous passageway we were met by women with scarlet hands – this was a paper making business.

Surrounded by huge vats of coloured dyes, they prepared trays of what looked like papier maché to dry in the sun- it was a dirty and smelly occupation, but I bought some of their cards and stationary which were quite unique.

Shortly after, we reached Tachapol Tol or Dattatraya Square the old centre of the town perhaps dating back to the eighth century.

It is lined by nine Hindu monasteries or 'math', which used to house religious communities of ascetics and yogis, but now mostly residences or handicraft shops.

One of the most famous stands behind the temple, this is the 15th century Pujari Math, restored with German funding for King Birendra.

It houses the Peacock Window, (a miniature copy of which I have in my front hall) and many carvings of cavorting wild boars, monkeys and 'makara', sea serpents.

Siddhi Lakshmi Temple (also known as the Lohan Dega or Stone Temple.)

A busy street side paper making factory run by women

Despite the messy production stages the end results were of a high quality

The 15th century Pujari Math building's 'Peacock Window', Bhaktapur

Miniature Copy

The Dattatraya Temple itself dating back to the 15th century was a former rest house for pilgrims and wandering sadhus. Erected in the reign of Yaksha Malla, the last king to rule from Bhaktapur, it

Nyatapola Temple

resembles the Kasthamandap of Kathmandu and is allegedly built from a single tree.

Dedicated to the three headed combination of Brahma, Vishnu and Shiva, it is guarded by gigantic statues of the Malla brothers. At the other end of the square was the local temple of Bhimsen, the patron saint of Newar merchants.

The true centre of Bhaktapur, Taumadhi Tol, was where we wandered to next – it was absolutely packed with people.

Dominating the skyline here is the 5-tiered Nyatapola Temple (98 feet high). Said to be the tallest in Nepal and poised atop a five-storey plinth, it honours an extremely secret Tantric form of the goddess Durga (Siddhi Lakshmi) who apparently has no devotees and has been barred to all, except priests, since it was built in 1702.

The 5 pairs of temple guardians lining the steep staircase are as famous as the temple itself.

First are the wrestling brothers, Jal and Patta Malla – who possessed the strength of ten men – followed by elephants, lions, griffons and two minor goddesses each said to be 10 times stronger than the last – the Bisket Jatra chariot with its solid wooden wheels was sitting beside the temple having been used recently.

Opposite, and completely contrasting, is the thick set Bhairabnath Mandir or Kasi Biswanath dedicated to a once unruly Bhairab whose legend tells of capture by priests who bound him by Tantric spells.

On trying to escape, they chopped off his head and he is now worshipped as a tiny 10 inch high gilded image which rides in the Bisket Jatra parade, every year.

Nearby is the 'dyochem' shrine of Betal, a hobgoblin who accompanies Bhairab on his annual chariot ride.

A troublesome being, he is worshipped for half-an-hour a year during the festival, while the rest of the time he is tied, facedown, to the topmost roof beams of his temple.

By this time, we were tired and hot from the hustle and bustle around us so we retired to the balcony of the Café Nyatapola, once a temple, with a cold beer where we could view the bands, celebrations and dancing at leisure.

Original Nepali artwork of street life

North of Tachapal (Dattatraya) is the area of Nawa Durga with a tantric temple which honours the nine manifestations of Durga.

This area occupies a special place in Bhaktapur's spiritual landscape and most famous of all are the Nawa Durga dancers, a troupe whose members are drawn from the caste of flower sellers. Each wears a heavy, painted clay mask which, empowered by tantric incantations, enables the wearer to become the very embodiment of the deity.

Every September a new set of masks are moulded and painted and on the 10th day of Dasain, the dancers and accompanying musicians dance their way to the 'Golden Gate' where they re-enact the legend of Durga's victory over a buffalo demon. We were taken to the small workshop to see how the masks were made and were able to buy miniature versions – I bought two, but only Ganesh survived.

On our way back to Kathmandu we stopped at the workshops on the outskirts of the town. Here we saw men making stunning brass buddhas: some producing the most intricate carving; young boys delicately painting the finest geometric thangkas ; and women along with babies and toddlers weaving the most beautifully patterned carpets.

We stopped off at a Tibetan village, as well, to see the spinning and weaving of a different type of carpet, again mostly woven by women – I only saw one man and he seemed to be supervising.

When we returned to the hotel I had a violent headache. The heat, dust and lack of food were the cause – some of our group had eaten at the café where we had a beer, but we had refrained from eating any food and I'm glad we did as one of our group caught 'campylobacter', only discovered when he returned home. We dined in our room that night and went to bed early.

Buddhist Village Craft Workshop

Carpet Weaving – Buddhist Village

Saturday 18th of April

I think we deserved a rest today so we rose late and walked down through the Thamel to do some shopping. In the afternoon Graham had a bone cracking massage from a man built like an ox, in the hotel spa.

At night we had a cooking demonstration and a late meal – altogether a much needed breathing space.

Sunday 19th of April

This morning we were to visit the town of Dhulikel to admire the view of the mountains, but the weather had changed. It was cloudy and thundery – the start of the monsoon was due any day – although we had been very lucky so far, this trip was cancelled.

After lunch, we visited Pashupatinath and Boudhanath. At the time I found it difficult to understand much of what was to be seen, but having travelled extensively since, I realise that everyone is entitled to their own faith and customs, no matter how unpalatable it would appear to me.

Pashupatinath (pronounced Posh-potty-not) is Nepal's holiest Hindu pilgrimage site and one of the most significant Shiva sites of the subcontinent, often compared to Varanasi in India. This sacred complex, littered with shrines, sculptures and statues, is a time-warp enclave of temples, cremation ghats, ritual bathers and half-naked Saddhus.

It all straddles the Bagmati River which is considered the most holy in Kathmandu Valley and this stretch the most sacred of all – Nepal's answer to India's sacred Ganges, in fact, the Bagmati is said to be connected to the Ganges by an underground stream.

Shiva is the main deity here in the form of Pashupati, 'Lord of the Beasts', in whose name praises are sung on Radio Nepal each morning. His symbolism appears everywhere in stone bulls representing his mount Nandi, in the trident, and ever present linga, his special symbol, representing the generative power of the universe.

Pashupatinath is situated on the eastern edge of Kathmandu, a short distance from the airport and, in winter, the horribly polluted river is barely a trickle, but the faithful still submerge themselves the prescribed three times and take a sip of the holy water.

For husbands and wives to bathe here together ensures that they will be remarried in the next life. To die and be cremated here is to be released from the cycle of rebirths according to tradition

We began our visit on the eastern bank where we could view the whole complex. According to legend it was here in the Mrigasthali Forest that Shiva once roamed as an antelope and where he lost his horn which was transformed into the powerful Pashupati 'linga'.

Several small temples and shrines sit on either side of the steps, all honouring Shiva and Lakshmi. These could be mistaken for tombs, but the statues of Nandi and Shiva and the 'linga' atop the 'yoni' proclaims them to be Shiva shrines.

Nearer the river are 11 great 'shivalaya' (shelters) erected in honour of women who committed 'sati' opposite on the funeral pyres of their husbands.

These provided shelter for the fluctuating population of Saddhus, wandering devotees who have renounced the strictures of caste and custom. These dreadlocked Saddhus either wear orange robes or smear their body with ashes from the cremation ghats.

They live by begging, are celibate and refrain from alcohol, but they consume huge quantities of 'ganja' (marijuana) under whose influence they often perform diverse contortions and mortifications of the flesh to free themselves from sensual passions.

Many are genuine devotees, but others are misfits or rogues who cannot fit into society in any other way. We saw a number always smiling and willing to pose for photographs, at a price. One we saw playing his pipe to charm snakes and a very sleepy cobra rose out of the basket – I think it must have been drugged or was half dead of hunger.

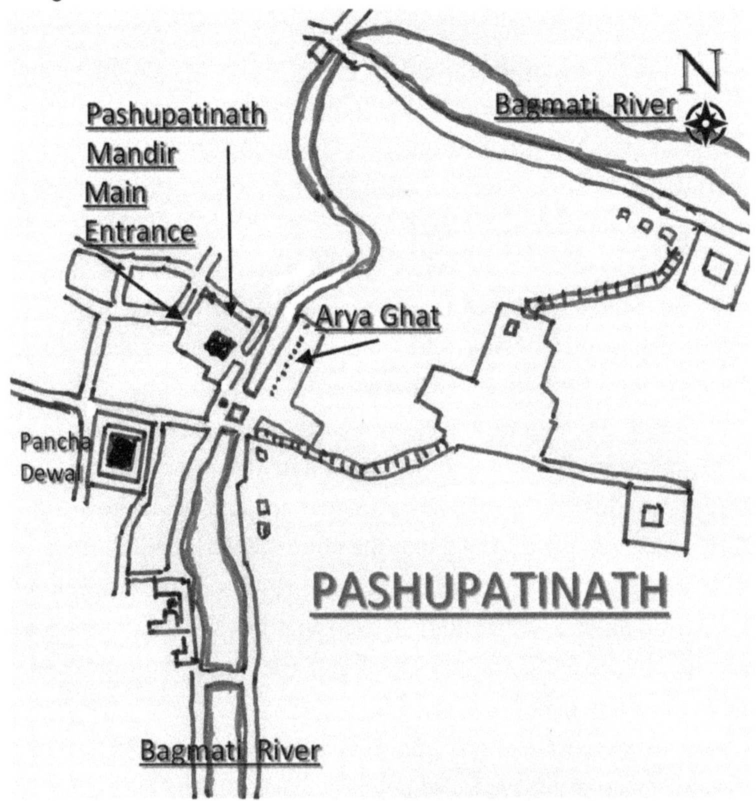

Map 15 Pashupatinath, Kathmandu

Crossing the narrow bridge spanning the Bagmati, we stopped to survey the scene.

Children were playing in the filthy river, and women were collecting bits of wood from the ashes, while fierce red-bottomed monkeys scampered around looking for food. Of course, cremations were continuing to be conducted by male relatives, with shaved heads and clad in white, a colour of mourning.

It was what faced me on the western bank that I found upsetting. All around the temple area are 'dharmsala' (pilgrims' rest houses) set aside for the devout and the dying. Those in their final hours were lying with their feet in the water and all over the streets there were sick people lying without care and attention – the smell was terrible, even our guide was affected.

Pashupatinath Views

The Pancha Dewal, whose five cupolas can be seen from the opposite bank, now serves as an old people's home, one wing of which is operated by Mother Theresa's Missionaries of Charity and here residents receive a good standard of care, but it is full to bursting.

More Pashupatinath Views

Making our way past trinket stalls , sweet shops and traders selling large amounts of brightly coloured powders – used to make the paints used in thangkas – we reached the Pashupati Mandir, the holy of holies for followers of Shiva.

The gold clad pagoda dates from the early 17th century but inscriptions indicate that a temple has been here since 477 AD, when the ancient village of Deopatan is said to have been founded. Over the years it has been constantly improved with gifts and donations, including doors of repoussé silver and a giant bull with silver hooves and a golden tail donated by a Rana Prime Minister as atonement for accidentally shooting a cow on a Terai hunt.

Like many orthodox temples, it is not open to non-Hindus, but nothing prevented us from having a look through the gate at the enormous brass backside of Nandi, Shiva's faithful bull. Hidden inside is the famous sacred black stone linga of Pashupatinath carved on four sides with a different aspect of Shiva.

During the 11th Century, the temple became a hotbed of tantric practices which continued for 400 years until King Yaksha Malla arranged for conventional Brahman priests from South India to take control. This continues until today as these orange clad holy men tend to the linga daily by washing, dressing and making offerings.

The scene was overwhelming and claustrophobic and our guide Henry, who had been bombarded by endless questions, led us up the hill to our coach. On the way a German chap stopped us and invited us in to have a drink – it was very hot and sultry. Little did we realise that this was a leper colony.

He must have seen the shock on our faces when faced with badly mutilated women and children, but he assured us that all had been cured and we could not catch the disease – old stigmas die hard.

The great stupa at Boudhanath, another holy site, was to be our next destination, only five minutes away.

Boudhanath

"- about three and a half miles From Kathmandu is a peculiar village called Bodhnath. This village is built in a circle round an immense temple

- This place is a favourite resort of the Bhotiyas and Tibetans who visit the valley in the cold season, and many of the houses are occupied as jewellers' shops wherein are manufactured peculiar amulets, armlets, necklaces et cetera which the Bhotiyas wear in great profusion,"

– ***Daniel Wright***, *History of Nepal,Delhi 1877*

Boudhanath is acknowledged to be the most important Buddhist monument outside Tibet. The 'Chorten Chempo' or "Great Stupa" has become a focal point for Tibetan refugees and a vibrant centre for

Buddhist teachings. As a result, the stupa is now engulfed by many new 'gompa' (monasteries) and carpet factories.

Historians are left at the mercy of legend, but its origins date back to the 5th Century AD. Tibetan legend tells how a lowly poultry keeper asked the local ruler for as much land as could be covered by the hide of a buffalo. However, she cleverly cut the skin into strips and used it to encircle a huge plot.

The king said something like "Permission once given cannot be taken back". To this day, Tibetans call this stupa, Jarung Kashor, basically what the king said.

Great importance is attached to this tale because it is attributed to Guru Padma Sambhava, Tibet's first ever and most beloved evangelist. Interestingly, in the same manuscript, the guru warns of an invasion by a giant enemy which would scatter the Tibetan people south into Nepal and India.

The Newar legend is more firmly grounded in history involving a drought that struck Kathmandu in the reign of Dharmadeva, a Licchavi King. Court astrologers advised that only the sacrifice of a virtuous man would bring rain. Dharmadeva ordered his son, Manadeva to behead a shrouded body near the royal well. He obeyed his father and carried out his gruesome task only to discover that the body was that of his own father. To allay his guilt he erected the Boudha Stupa.

View from the Boudhanath Stupa

The Buddhist stupa has evolved from burial tumuli of ancient India and often enshrines sacred relics. Its components represent the cosmos: the base represents earth; the dome water; the spire fire; the tip air and the 'bindu' topmost point, ether. The 13- storeyed, gilded spire symbolises the stages to enlightenment. Boudhanath embodies a giant mandala, with a rounded dome set on stepped square plinths.

Boudhanath

View from Boudhanath

A uniquely, Nepali touch are the eyes painted on the base of the spire with varying expressions or, as some say, 'all knowing'.

Some say they are Buddha's eyes, whilst others believe they are more associated with the protective eyes painted on buildings all over Kathmandu.

The Nepalese number '1', a graceful squiggle, serves as the nose of the face and the reminder of unity.

The huge whitewashed dome of Boudhanath is said to enshrine the relics of Kasyapa, a leading disciple of Buddha.

Buddhists consider it to be an extraordinarily powerful site able to fulfil wishes and, as a result, pilgrims from many parts pay homage here.

View from Boudhanath

We climbed the stairs leading up to the tiered base above which rises the 13 golden steps to 'nirvana'. The topmost level circles the stupa itself, its base being inset with 108 niches each containing ancient stone images of the deities. Returning down, we saw a small whitewashed building housing a shrine to an eighth Century tantric wizard, Guru Rinpoche, its old frescoes stained by the soot from the constant flickering butter lamps.

Opposite, built into the wall, is the small Ajuna shrine sheltering the image of a nasty goddess dining on a hapless victim. Gruesome though she may look, Newari Buddhists worship her as a grand-mother – protectress of children, also known as Harati, the goddess of smallpox.

Nearby is a gigantic prayer -wheel where all are welcome to spin. Once outside the gate we joined the clockwise ritual of circumambulation and the spinning prayer wheels alongside the chanting and praying monks, nuns and regular devotees – a fitting end to the afternoon.

Tonight, there was to be a reception and dinner in a hotel called Dwarika's – we had no idea what to expect. We arrived at a wooden door located in a long, high wall, which didn't look very promising, but once inside we discovered an architectural gem.

Dwarikas has become an asylum and hospital for the care of wounded masterpieces in wood, where they are restored to their original beauty, a school for training practise of traditional arts and skills, a laboratory to research old techniques and a living museum where people may enjoy and understand the Nepali heritage.

"Hotel Heritage – Dwarika's Kathmandu Hotel, it took eight centuries and twenty eight years to build."

- ***Sonam Tashi***

Everywhere the Newari craft of woodcarving can be seen – in doors, window frames, arches and balconies. This unique hotel is set in an old garden filled with fruit trees, lawns, fountains and small streams.

It was all begun by Dwarika Das Shrestha who scoured the alleys and courtyards all over the Kathmandu valley picking up a door here and a window there, saving whatever he could of the old architectural pieces. Building a Hotel was the only logical way forward, with his horde of woodcraft and it would provide funds to continue preservation work.

After being shown around by Rajesh and told of the many important previous guests, such as Prince Charles, the Clintons and various European princes and princesses, we were taken to the Astamangal Bar where we were introduced to raksi.

This is a locally-made liquor distilled from Kodo (millet). It was served slightly warm in small clay dishes and accompanied by 'dalmut', spicy deep-fried lentils mixed with peanuts and peas.

Next we were ushered to the Krishnarpan, a special Nepalese restaurant in a beautiful and historic setting. We dined at a long table designed with centuries-old woodwork, sat on silk cushions (once our shoes had been removed) and ate and drank from years old traditional plates, bowls and glasses.

Courtyard Of Dwarika's Hotel –
including some of the reclaimed window frames on the 1st floor

The girls who served us were dressed in marriage costumes of red and gold. As our aprons were tied on and we were handed out personalised six course menus we realised that this was not just a meal but an experience itself of Nepalese hospitality and style.

We ate pancakes stuffed with lentils and cheese; fresh fish, mushrooms and red bean curry; vegetable soup; lamb with tomato spinach,

Dwarika Pre Dinner Drinks

Dwarika's Krishnarpan Restaurant

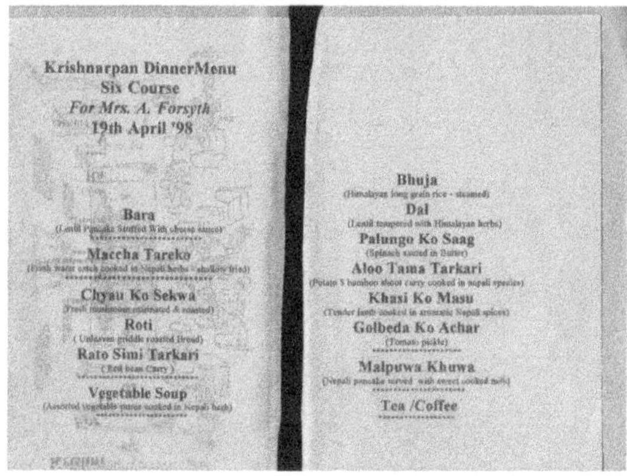

Krishnarpan DinnerMenu
Six Course
For Mrs. A. Forsyth
19th April '98

Bara
(Lentil Pancake Stuffed With cheese sauce)

Maccha Tareko
(Fresh water catch cooked in Nepali herbs - shallow fried)

Chyau Ko Sekwa
(Fresh mushroom marinated & roasted)

Roti
(Unleaven griddle roasted bread)

Rato Simi Tarkari
(Red bean Curry)

Vegetable Soup
(Assorted vegetable puree cooked in Nepali herb)

Bhuja
(Himalayan long grain rice - steamed)

Dal
(Lentil tempered with Himalayan herbs)

Palungo Ko Saag
(Spinach sauted in Butter)

Aloo Tama Tarkari
(Potato & bamboo shoot curry cooked in nepali species)

Khasi Ko Masu
(Tender lamb cooked in aromatic Nepali spices)

Golbeda Ko Achar
(Tomato pickle)

Malpuwa Khuwa
(Nepali pancake served with sweet cooked milk)

Tea /Coffee

Audrey's Dwarika Dinner Menu

potato and rice and finally a Nepali pancake with sweet cooked milk – it was all delicious.

Coffee and more raksi followed to end a very enjoyable evening.

The Nepali journey nears its end

Farewell to the majestic Himalaya

Nepal – a country and people left but not forgotten

Monday 20th of April

Breakfast, last-minute shopping and packing occupied the early morning. At about 1:30 pm we set off for the airport to check in with P I A. The sky was black, thunder boomed and lightning flashed as the torrential monsoon rain poured down. Our guide told us that the mountains were crying because we were leaving.

Once aboard the plane, the first of our problems began – the engines of the plane would not start. We had to sit in sweltering heat as they procured a 'start-cart' from the adjoining domestic airport and then we were off and on our way to Karachi in Pakistan where we were to spend the night.

Arriving at 9:00 pm we were struck with the hot, humid air as soon as we exited the airport building. Our flight tickets were reconfirmed, but we were required to leave our large luggage and passports at the airport – apparently part of the regulations for a short stay.

The evening drive through the streets of Karachi was interesting as we passed many decorated and colourful buses and rows and rows of wedding parlours lit up and full of people, until we reached the Hotel Marriot.

It was a beautiful hotel with a large plush reception and armed guards stationed all around – a bit disconcerting. Our room was pleasant and, even although a wedding was proceeding at the nearby poolside, we were so exhausted that we fell asleep immediately.

Tuesday 21st of April

We rose early and then went down to breakfast. It was so hot and humid that, even with air conditioning working, Graham's shirt was soaked through in a few minutes. Our itinerary today included a short city tour of Karachi, before going to the airport for our PIA flight to London at 2:30 pm.

Masjid e Tooba Mosque

Mr Khan, a pleasant gentleman, indicated certain points of interest as we drove through the busy city streets.

Many of the old buildings were British, before Independence, especially the churches and cemeteries. We passed the Iranian Library and the striking Mohatta Palace, built in the tradition of the stone palaces in Rajasthan, using pink Jodhpur stone in combination with the local yellow stone from Gizri.

Our first stop was at the Mazar-e-Quaid, the Jinnah Mausoleum or the National Mausoleum of the founder of Pakistan, Muhammad Ali Jinnah. This iconic symbol of Karachi, in Sindh Province, was completed in the 1960s at the heart of the city. Used for official and military ceremonies, the mausoleum, designed by Yahya Merchant, is made of white marble with curved Moorish arches and sits on an elevated platform.

In each wall is placed an entrance, and 15 successive fountains lead to one entrance with terraced avenues on all the others. The cool interior was very welcome as the temperature had already reached 45°C – although we were almost knocked over by the soldiers during the changing of the guard.

On our way again we passed by the river where thousand of washing lines fluttered in the wind. This was the home of the Dhobi Wallahs who collected and returned laundry in their many donkey carts. Soon we were standing by the Arabian Sea, at Clifton beach, where the blustery wind almost sent us skyward.

There were a few families on the beach, but instead of donkeys, many camels were ready to ply their trade. Past Benazir Bhutto's house (palace), we came to the Masjid e Tooba, often claimed to be the largest single domed mosque in the world.

Made of white marble, the dome is 236 feet in diameter and is balanced on a low surrounding wall with no central pillars. The acoustics inside, I can attest, are quite amazing – a normal speaking voice in the centre can be heard easily at any point in the mosque.

Our last stop was the obligatory carpet shop where they also sold quite stunning onyx-ware, but we had no Pakistani money – these were the days before credit cards.

After a quick return to the hotel for our hand luggage, we set off for Jinnah International Airport and our journey home – or so we thought! Our first blow turned out to be that the flight was delayed until 4:30 pm, but the worst was still to come.

A problem had arisen with our seat bookings in relation to the first leg of our London flight which had started from Islamabad before coming to Karachi.

It turned out that there were insufficient seats left for the whole party to fly as a group and therefore we had to stay overnight in Karachi in order to get a plane next day.

This was not entirely straightforward as it turned out. We had retired to a hotel accommodation overnight having been told our flight was 7:00am next morning.

After an exhausting day we eventually got to sleep at about midnight only to be telephoned and rudely awakened just after 1:00 am to be advised that our flight was leaving at 3:00am and to get down to the hotel entrance area – where transport was waiting – as soon as possible.

After a sudden rush to the airport and boarding at around 2.30am it was not until we were about to take off that we found we were actually on a flight north to the city of Lahore.

We arrived there still early in the morning and from there we then got a flight back to London. It was a cramped flight which flew directly over Iraq.

At the London Heathrow luggage collection area we waited and waited for our luggage among the TV sets, cricket bats, and crates of oranges on the carousel but soon found out that our luggage was still in Pakistan. Here, too, the SAGA tour representative who met us was useless and could only tell us that they had lost us for 3 days- all of which we knew.

British Midland was wonderful when they heard our tale of woe and they gave us access to the executive lounge prior to a quick flight home. Our luggage arrived two days later.

-ooOoo-

Modern History Of Nepal

Timeline (Source BBC website)

1768	Ruler Prithvi Narayan Shah takes over Kathmandu Valley and starts to unify the country
1814-16	Anglo-Nepalese War ends in a Treaty and existing country boundaries
1846	Ranas dominate the monarchy and isolate the country from the outside world
1923	Treaty with Britain - sovereignty retained
1951	End of Rana rule. Crown restored
1953	Edmund Hillary and Sherpa Tenzing Norgay first climbers to reach summit of Mount Everest
1955	Nepal joins United Nations
1955	King Tribhuwan dies and King Mahendra takes over
1959	Multiparty constitution introduced
1960	King Mahendra takes over control and suspends parliament after B P Koirali wins election
1962	King introduces non party punchayet system of councils
1972	King Mahendra dies - succeeded by King Bivendra
1980	King agrees to allow direct election on a non party basis
1985	Disobedience campaign introduced for the restoration of multi party politics
1986	New elections boycotted
1989	Economy dives due to a trade dispute with India
1990	After pro-democracy agitation King Birendra agrees to a new Democratic constitution
1991	After elections G P Koirala becomes PM
1994	P M Koirali's Government defeated and communist government formed after election
1995	Communist government dissolved
1995	Start of Maoist revolt which continued for over 10 years
1997	Period of government instability
2000	GP Koirala returns as P M
2001	Palace massacre -Crown Prince Dipendra kills King Birendra and Queen Aishwarya before taking his own life. Gyanendra is crowned King.
2001	Maoist violence increases. GP Koirala leaves. Sher Bahadur Deuba takes over
2001	State of emergency declared after Maoist violence increases

2002	Parliament dissolved, and after new elections held Sher Bahadur Deuba renews Emergency but is later dismissed.
2003	Rebels and government declares ceasefire
2003	Peace talks breakdown
2005	King Gyanendra dismisses government and restores absolute monarchy and declares a state of emergency
2005	Parliament restored
2006	Parliament curb's King Gyanendra's powers. Peace talks held with Maoists. Peace deal signed.
2007	Maoists join government
2007	Violence erupts. Parliament agrees to abolish the monarchy as part of the peace deal
2008	Nepal becomes a Republic
2008	Ram Baran Yadav becomes the first President of Nepal

NOTES *

Note 1. 1st June 2001
Nepalese Royal Palace Massacre

This massacre took place at a house in the grounds of the Narayanhity Royal Palace in central Kathmandu.

Nine members of the royal family were killed in a mass shooting which took place during a party which had taken the form of a monthly reunion dinner of the royal family.

King Birendra of Nepal and Queen Aishwarya and a further 7 members of the royal family died in the mass shooting carried out by their son, Crown Prince Dipendra.

He had slipped into a coma after shooting himself and died three days later. Birendra's brother Gyanendra then became king.

Note 2. 23rd December 2007
Political Change / Abolition Of The Monarchy

The constitutional monarchy with King Gyanendra reign ended in 2008 when the Constitution was altered to make the country a republic.

The king had suspended Parliament earlier in 2002 and appointed a government led by himself enforcing martial law at a time when the Maoist insurgency was taking place.

A countryside uprising against the King's autocratic rule, involving all political parties, resulted in a return to total legislative and executive Parliamentary powers with agreement for the monarchy to be abolished taken on 23rd of December 2007

Note 3. 25th of April 2015
Nepal Earthquake Damage

This shallow earthquake had an epicentre just 60 km north-west of the Nepali capital, Kathmandu.

Destruction was widespread, as was loss of life, it being the worst earthquake in Nepal in more than 80 years.

Hundreds of thousands of people in chilling conditions were made homeless with entire areas completely flattened and harvests substantially reduced or lost.

Being a hilly country, the steep valleys suffered many landslides with Ghodatabela Village covered in one of these slides, killing around 250 people.

It is estimated that 8,632 people died and a further 19,009 people were injured in the quake.

Many of the centuries old buildings and temple structures were destroyed in many of the UNESCO World lHeritage sites in the Kathmandu Valley area including some parts of the Changu Narayan location, a Temple visited by Audrey.

Photo 1
Earthquake Damage Kathmandu

Photo 2
Bhaktapur Durbar Square

Thousands of domestic homes were also destroyed. Photos below are examples of the horrendous damage produced by the Nepal earthquake as it affected Kathmandu and the Basantapur Square and also Bhaktapur Durbar Square areas. The Boudhanath Stupa was also affected by the earthquake.

Photo 3 – Basantapur Square, Kathmandu

Photo 4 – Bhaktapur Durbar Square

Note 4 – 25th April 2015
Nepal Earthquake Mount Everest

Everest was not immune to this earthquake either. Its effect was to trigger an avalanche killing approximately 20 people.

Note 5 -25th September 2011
Buddha Air plane crash

On the 25th of September 2011 Buddha Air flight 103, similar to the plane we had used, crashed near Lalitpur (Patan) in Nepal while attempting to land in poor weather killing all 19 passengers and crew on board. This aircraft had also been on a sightseeing flight to Mount Everest.

General Glossary of Nepali and Tibetan Words

Including Deities & Place Names

Nepali and Tibetan Words

avatar	incarnation or manifestation of a deity
bahal	Newari Buddhist monastery complex
baksheesh	a tip; often a bribe
bhajan	religious hymn
Bhaktapur	city of devotees
Bhotia, Bhotiya, Bhotey,	general term for Tibetan-influenced people of the northern border regions
bodhisattva	a buddha-to-be who has renounced individual enlightenment to help other beings
chaitya	a Buddhist monument, a miniature version of a stupa
chang	home-made beer, usually brewed from barley
chautara	shady trailside resting place with a low wall to support porters' loads
chorten	a small stupa, sometimes with a passage through the middle so that people can walk through it
chowk	a square or courtyard
dal bhat	The national dish of Nepal: lentils (dal) and cooked rice (bhat),served with curried vegetables
dhara	water tap
didi	older sister
doko	wicker basket used for carrying loads
dorje	see vojra
dyochem	(Newari) 'god's house', a special shrine
gainey	a minstrel caste
ghat	flight of stone steps lining river banks, used for laundry, bathing and cremation
gompa	Tibetan Buddhist monastery
guthi	traditional Newari social association

hiti	sunken fountain typical of the Kathmandu Valley
jatra	festival
Kathmandu	from Kasthamandap which stood in Durbar Square. Kastha means wood and Mandapa means Pavilion ie a rest house
khukri	Curved Nepali knife
kora	circumambulation
Kot	the Royal Palace Armory
Kumari	young virgin Buddhist girl worshipped as a manifestation of the Hindu goddess Durga
ladoo	a milk-based sweet
lama	guru; religious teacher
Licchavi	a ruling dynasty of the Kathmandu Valley (ad 300-879)
linga	symbol related to Shiva and the phallus
mdkara	sea serpents of Hindu mythology
malla	wrestler
mandala	mystic diagram depicting the order of the universe
mani	prayer wall: heap of flat stones engraved with mantra and religious images, found in mountainous Buddhist regions
mantra	mystic formula of Sanskrit syllables
math	Hindu monastery
mela	fair, often associated with a religious festival
momo	meat-stuffed dumplings
maovad dwandakaal	the Nepal civil war
mudra	symbolic gestures
naga	serpent deities: guardians of wealth associated with rain
namaste	I salute the god within you
Narayanhiti	name of the royal palace in Kathmandu. The name comprises two words – Narayana , the hindu god Vishnu whose temple is opposite and hiti meaning water spout in Newar language, which is situated to the east of the main entrance in the palace precincts.
Nepalese Civil War	also known as the Maoist conflict or insurgency was a war fought between the Communist Party of Nepal (Maoist) and the government of Nepal from 1996 to 2006.

Newar	The Newar people were the historical inhabitants of Kathmandu
Parvati	Shiva's spouse
Pashupati	early incarnation of Shiva as the lord of the beast
Patan	old city in Kathmandu valley also called Lalitpur meaning Beautiful city
Panchayat	the political system of Nepal from 1960 to 1990. A system of self governance - party less - historically prevalent in the Indian subcontinent.
pati	open rest-house providing shelter to travellers
puja	ritual gift and prayer
rakshi	(Tibetan, arak) potent alcoholic beverage distilled from grain
sal	hardwood tree (Shorea robusta) famed for its fine-grained wood
samsara	the cycle of delusion created by the unenlightened mind
sadhu	Hindu ascetic or holy man
Shakti	a cosmic energy in female form
shikhara	a tapered tower surmounting a temple
shikar	the hunt
sindhur	red powder used as religious offering
sirdar	organiser of a trek or expedition
stupa	Buddhist monument: a hemispheric mound topped by a conical spire
tantra	school of mysticism developed in medieval India which has influenced both Hinduism and Buddhism
terai	grassland and marsh belt - northern most limit of the floodplain of the Ganges River (the holiest river for a hindu), is the most fertile part of the country producing 60% of the grain for the nation
tempo	three-wheeled motor vehicle serving as an inexpensive public taxi
thangka	(Tibetan) scroll painting depicting religious subjects
tika	auspicious mark on the forehead, made as part of worship
tol	neighbourhood or quarter of a city

tongba	drink made from hot water mixed with fermented mash
torana	semicircular carved tympanum mounted over temple doors and windows
topi	Nepali men's cap, brimless and slightly lopsided
tsampa	roasted barley flour, a highland staple
tuk tuk	motorised rickshaw
yaksha	graceful nymph of Hindu mydiology
vojra	Buddhist ritual implement representing the absolute aspect of reality

-ooOoo-

Hindu and Buddhist Deities

Ajima	Newari grandmother goddesses; indigenous deities often placated with blood sacrifice
Annapurna	goddess of the harvest, a manifestation of Lakshmi
Ashta Matrika '	Eight Mothers, each representing a different aspect of Durga
Avalokitesvara	compassionate Bodhisattva who grew eleven heads and 1,000 arms in order to help suffering beings; see Lokesvara
Bhagwati	another name for the goddess Durga
Bhairab	fierce manifestation of Shiva
Bhimsen	patron god of traders: a minor figure in the Mahabharata
Bisket Jatra	festival where the god Bhairab and his wife Bhadrakala are dragged on a trailer through the streets.
Buddha	an enlightened being; more particularly the historical Buddha, Siddhartha Gautama
Brahma	known as the hindu creator god who is supreme in the Hindu triad gods of Shiva and Vishnu.
Bunga Dyo	local name for Machhendranath
Chamunda	who holds the power over death
Chandeswari	fierce goddess associated with Durga, slayer of the demon Chand
Devi	another name for the goddess Durga or Parvati
Durga	The Great Goddess, appearing in many different forms, but most popularly as the defeater of the evil buffalo demon Mahisasura.
Ganesh	is the elephant-headed god of luck who is the son of Shiva and Parvati
Ganga	goddess associated with the sacred River Ganges, usually appearing with Jamuna, the personification of another sacred Indian river
Garuda	is a legendary winged man and is the mount of Vishnu
Goraknath	12th-century yogi deified as an aspect of Shiva
Guru Rinpoche	***see*** Padmasambhava

Guyheswari	the Secret Goddess, a name for Shiva's spouse Sati
Hanuman	the Monkey King, a prominent figure in the *Ramayana*, worshipped as a protector
Indra	Vedic deity honoured as King of the Gods
Kali	the 'Black One' a hideous goddess personifying death
Krishna	blue-complexioned god of love, an incarnation of Vishnu
Kumari	young virgin worshipped as an incarnation of Durga
Lakshmi	goddess of wealth and abundance who is the consort of Vishnu
Lokesvara	(Lokeswar, Karunamaya) 'Lord of the World', beloved bodhisattva and god of compassion
Machhendranath	rainmaking patron deity of the Kathmandu Valley, worshipped primarily by the Buddhist Newars
Mai	indigenous deities transformed into 'Mother Goddesses', usually associated with a particular locality
Manjushri	bodhisattva and embodiment of wisdom and learning Nandi mount of Shiva, depicted as a kneeling bull
Nandi	the white bull ridden by Shiva
Narasimha	incarnation of Vishnu, half man, half lion
Padmapani	lotus-holding bodhisattva; see Lokesvara
Padmasambhava	Indian tantric responsible for the introduction of Buddhism into Tibet
Pancha Buddha	five Buddhas, each associated with a different element, colour, direction and aspect of enlightenment
Parvati	consort of Shiva and a goddess in her own right
Pashupati(nath)	Lord of the Beasts, benevolent form of Shiva
Saraswati	goddess of learning and culture
Siddhartha Gautama	original buddhist leader
Shiva	important Hindu deity – both a transformer and destroyer
Sitala	goddess of smallpox and protector of children; Newari Buddhists worship her as Harati

Stupa	a dome-shaped building erected as a Buddhist shrine
Sutala	***see*** Sitala
Taleju	tantric goddess imported from India and made patron of the Malla dynasty; related to Durga
Tara	(Tibetan Dolma) female bodhisattva represents mercy and appears in 21 forms the most important is the White and Green Taras
Vajra Yogini	Tantric Buddhist deity, a fierce protector goddess
Vishnu	an important Hindu god worshipped as the Preserver who appears in 10 principal incarnations

-ooOoo-

Nepal Geographic Terms Place Names

Alaya	dwelling place
Ban	forest
Bazaar	market area or market town aka Bajar, Bazar
Besi	a lower village or bazaar associated with a particular place
Bhanjyang	pass or ridge top
Bhatti	tea shop, restaurant, traditional inn or guest house in the hills
Chaur	flat meadow or campsite (western Nepal)
Chautaara	trailside rock wall and ledge built as a resting place for porters
Chhahara	waterfall
Chomolungma	Mount Everest (Tibetan) goddess of the wind, mother earth
Chorten	stone Buddhist monument, usually rounded
Chowk	courtyard or square at a road intersection
Chu	river or body of water (Tibetan)
Dakshin	south
Danda	hill or ridge in mid hills aka Daanda
Deorali	ridge top
Dhara	waterspout
Dharmsala	pilgrim's resthouse
Dingma	clearing (Tibetan)
Dhoka	gate
Drangka	minor stream
Durbar	palace or noble
Dzong	fort, fortified monastery or palace (Tibetan)
Everest	Mountain 29,028ft (8848m) high – Earth's highest mountain. The international border between Nepal and China runs across its summit point. Named in 1865 by the British Royal Geographical Society after a previous British Surveyor of India – Sir George Everest – see Chomolungma and Sagarmatha
Gaad	river (western Nepal)
Gandaki	river
Ganga	river, sacred river of Nepal

Gaon	village aka Gaau
Ghar	house
Ghat	riverside place for cremations
Ghatte	water mill
Ghunsa	winter settlement (Tibetan)
Gompa	Bhuddist temple (Tibetan)
Goth	high altitude cowshed or herdsman's hut
Haat	market or hill bazaar (eastern Nepal)
Himal	Sanscrit word for snow mountain
JhochhemTole	named Freak Street after the hippie trail of 1960s and 1970s.
Kang	Beauty, also another name of the Hindu god Lakshmi
Kanti	Mountain
Kharka	high altitude communal pasture (usually for yaks or yak-cow hybrids)
Khola	river or stream
Kosi	major river (seven in Nepal)
Kot	fortress
Kund	holy lake
La	high mountain pass (Tibetan)
Lagna	ridge or pass (western Nepal) aka Laagna
Lekh	ridge or high area in mid hills
Lho	south (Tibetan)
Mandir	temple
Margway	e.g. Durbar Marg The Kings Way
Mela	country fair
Middle Hills	Also known as the Mahabharat range and the Churia Hills is the topographical region between the Himalaya and the Terai
Nadi	small stream or minor river (Hindi)
Nag Hrad	tank of serpents
Nala	small stream (Naalaa)
Nup	west (Tibetan)
Parbat	mountain
Pashchin	west

Phedi	lower. Used to denote a nearby settlement at the bottom of a mountain, or the bottom of a mountain itself
Pokhari	lake or large water tank
Pul	bridge
Purba	east
Ri	peak or mountain (Tibetan)
Saano	small
Sagarmatha	Mount Everest (Nepal) sky's head, mother earth
Sangu	bridge (western Nepal)
Shar	east (Tibetan)
Tal	lake aka Taal
Tatopani	hot spring
Thanga	riverside
Thanti	a place
Thulo	big
Tole	street or quarter of a town or village
Tsho	lake (Tibetan)
Tundikhel	an open space for practicing archery and martial sports, as well as an official parade ground.
Uttar	north
Yarsa	crop field above village summer ground

-ooOoo

Acknowledgements

- **Posthumously To Audrey** – Mine has been an entirely support role in adding the presentation aspects, photographs and book format to the complete text manuscript that she had completed.

I know that she was methodical in checking all her facts and completed that to the very best of her ability. In acquiring these facts I know that she endeavoured also not to infringe any copyright issues.

This was a task completed by her primarily to generate a library of books, of which this is but one, in the knowledge that the travel experiences and locations she had had the good fortune to visit and which, in the fullness of time may not all survive as she had known them, but that her books would provide a descriptive and pictorial record that our grandchildren, when older, could read, learn from and enjoy.

It also provides a similar opportunity for adults with a curiosity surrounding travel to enjoy these as well.

Accordingly it would be remiss of me, as her husband, and having seen at first hand the enormous effort it took for her to complete these texts at a time when her health was sadly deteriorating, not to acknowledge her sacrifice and ultimate achievement. She was a fighter as well as having a talented mind.

-

- **To Kim and Sinclair Macleod** from Indie Authors World, indieauthorsworld.com, for their constructive and supportive comments and helpful advice to me in putting these texts into book form.

-

- **To our 6 grandchildren and two bumps** that Audrey knew but which I have come to know as 8 young individual and curious persons whom I love so much and to whom these books are dedicated..

-

- **To the people of Nepal** to thank them for their hospitality and friendship.

List Of Individual Maps

This is the first in a *Tales Of A Grandmother* book series which are the produce of the late Audrey Forsyth.

In these she shares and brings to life her travel experiences and love of language, culture, history , music and people.

A 25% share of book proceeds is donated to the charity Pancreatic Cancer Uk to help fund life-saving research.

Pancreatic cancer.org.uk

For Readers' Information

'Nepal' is Audrey's first book published in

her Tales Of A Grandmother series.

Her second Tales Of A Grandmother book, soon to be published, is……

'A Trip Around The Black Sea'.

-Not to be missed!

And other Tales Of A Grandmother books

in preparation and to follow on are……

South America

Russian River Cruise

Cultural Turkey

- All are interesting, diverse, enlightening and unique -

Further Up-to-date Information is available

on the Tales Of A Grandmother website.
talesofagrandmother.com

Enjoy.

"Travel makes one modest. You see what a tiny place you occupy in the world" – Gustave Flaubert

Lightning Source UK Ltd.
Milton Keynes UK
UKHW021004170121
377164UK00006B/23

9 781838 308803